D1242470

God,
Man
and
Archie
Bunker

God, Man And Archie Bunker

SPENCER MARSH

Foreword by Carroll O'Connor

HARPER & ROW PUBLISHERS
New York Evanston
San Francisco London

ISBN: 0-06-065423-6

ISBN: 0-06-065422-8 paper

LIBRARY OF CONGRESS CATALOG CARD NUMBER: 74-25694

Designed by C. Linda Dingler

75 76 77 78 79 10 9 8 7 6 5 4 3 2

*This book is dedicated to four beautiful
women whom I love dearly:
Doris, Wendy, Sharee, Julie*

ALL IN THE FAMILY

Contributing Writers

NORMAN LEAR
DON NICHOLL
MICHAEL ROSS
BERNIE WEST

TOM & HELEN AUGUST
VINCENT BOGERT
ROBERT FISHER
SUSAN HARRIS
BRYAN JOSEPH
LEE KALCHEIM
ALLAN KATZ
ARTHUR MARX
JERRY MAYER
PHILIP MISHKIN
TINA & LES PINE
ROB REINER
DON REO
SANDY STERN
BURY STYLER
PAUL WAYNE

Contents

viii

Foreword

Recently on television I heard Dick Cavett ask George Meany what he thought of Archie Bunker. The great labor leader replied that the character was a bigot and a slander against the American working man. The conversation veered away, and Mr. Meany had left the impression that he thinks of "All in the Family" as antilabor. He does not, really. He has himself told me how much he enjoys the show. What he meant, I am sure, is that it would be slanderous of us—of the show—to present Archie Bunker as the typical American worker. To that, no argument.

From the beginning we have worked on the characterization of one man, a unique man, and his family. We never wanted to typify. Typifying is a function of the sociologist; it is a scientific job, somebody else's job. If audiences were to find anything typical in what we performed, let them conjure it themselves, not turn up something we actually planted.

Naturally Archie had to live somewhere and had to be something, but we hoped our choices would not be taken as generalizations. When Norman Lear and I first began talking about a pilot show in the summer of 1968 we considered all regional possibilities, but we decided to follow the lead of the hit British comedy " 'Til Death Us Do Part," which Norman had transferred to America. That is to say, the counterpart of London is New York, so we fixed on New York; and that being our locale, it remained for us to construct a character-counterpart of the Cockney Alf Garnett. But if Archie was to be a New Yorker, we believed then as now that he was equally alive and well in Tulsa, Denver, and Des Moines.

We followed the working-man image created on the British show, though we were not bound to it. It is hard after five strongly etched seasons to think of Archie as anything but his established self, yet the voices of bigotry, racism, superpatriotism, and ignorant prejudice—the voices of Archie Bunker—speak ominously and hilariously along every walk of life, high, middle, or low. So Archie the urban worker was also, and is, a farmer, a civil servant, a professional man, an industrialist, a financier. We could have put him anywhere because he is a part of everywhere. We could have made him anyone because he is a part of everyone.

But everyone is not a part of him. That is his trouble. That is also why he is not typical: not your typical working man, nor any other sort of man, nor even (thanks be to God) your typical American.

Nor is he an updated Everyman, as some writer identified him. Today's Everyman, morally and intellectually (and typically), is on the move. Archie seems to be moving not at all. Today's Everyman, though not as enlightened as he should be, is better informed than Archie. For instance, he is beginning to investigate his society and to know his friends from his enemies. Archie is still blind to social menace so long as the flag is slickly wrapped round it and a demagogue consecrates it with a slogan. Take war. Everyman is beginning to understand that war, every war, is the ultimate, horrible failure of faulty systems and fraudulent men, "ours" as well as "theirs." But Archie still sees war simplistically as angry Justice annihilating Evil—and Evil is always foreign.

Everyman may still harbor doubts about racial equality, but his mind is opening a little. He no longer propounds his own superiority. He may oppose mixed marriage for his children, but he no longer rails publicly against the concept. He is still in an elementary stage of reeducation; but consider Archie, who will today tell you that the white race courts dark peril by sharing anything more than breathing space with the other races of man. Everyman is far ahead of Archie.

And Archie still sees the Almighty as a God of wrath to be fearfully obeyed. Everyman is beginning to believe in God as Love. Therein lies perhaps the most striking difference between Everyman and Archie: a spirit that grows brighter as opposed to a spirit that remains glum. Everyman is happier than Archie.

Given such differences, how then explain the responsive chord evoked everywhere by Archie's spiritual and temporal shenanigans? Why have 50 to 60 percent of all Saturday night television viewers enjoyed Archie for so long?

The answer, I think, is that Everyman, when he looks at Archie, knows that he is not looking at himself; he is happily looking back at what he was. Our author, Reverend Marsh, sees repentance in this, and he is probably right. I see relief, because though repentance and relief are closely related, there is more solemnity in the former and more laughter in the latter.

As I am writing these lines—it is the morning of December

27, 1974—the radio is announcing the death of one of our most enthusiastic fans, Jack Benny. When I last spoke to that sweet prince of entertainers, he said, "Your show is wonderful, it gives us all so much to think about." And I recalled Norman Lear's promise six years earlier: "We may be thrown off the air, but while we're there we'll give them plenty to think about." That is all he had in mind, all any of us had in mind.

But that, in the television industry, was a revolutionary and all but unattainable goal—the stimulation of serious social thought through comedy! I think it must be Norman's greatest pride, in which we all share, that he achieved his goal.

Part of the evidence of that achievement is this very book—this most thoughtful book—by Spencer Marsh.

CARROLL O'CONNOR

Los Angeles, California

Preface

I am not much fun on Saturday night. I don't know if it is true of all preachers, but for years I have anticipated my Sunday morning sermon in much the same way as a boxer waits in the dressing room for his call to enter the ring. These last couple of years, however, things have improved. I have found a remedy for my Saturday night tension in a TV program entitled "All in the Family."

It is therapeutic because it makes me laugh out most of my anxieties. Though I must admit that some of my laughter puzzles me, I have discovered, in studying my puzzlement, that the laughter is generally healthy. When I see my own foolishness in the various characters in the show I end up laughing at myself, which I think is good. Being able to laugh at oneself may just be the beginning of repentance, and in our society a little repentance couldn't hurt anyone.

There are other times when I am constrained to stop in the middle of a laugh and say, "That isn't funny; it's the kind of thing that's going to lead us to our destruction." In this way the show often brings us to our senses. And that's what the present book is all about—laughter, repentance, and coming to our senses.

This book happened because of the initial encouragement of a beautiful human being by the name of Jean Stapleton; the graciousness of a most unique, concerned, and dedicated man, Norman Lear; the cooperation of his most able and supportive staff assistant, Virginia Carter. I thank them all, and that gifted actor, Carroll O'Connor, whose talent and life-style I much admire.

SPENCER MARSH

God,
Man
and
Archie
Bunker

1

Archie's God

"In the beginning Archie created God in his own image. In his own image created he him."

The major difference between this paraphrase and the original in the first chapter of Genesis is that God and man, in this case Archie Bunker, have switched positions. It sounds weird, like the clay forming the potter, the bat swinging the batter, or the horn playing the blower. But strange as it sounds, the God of Archie Bunker was created by Archie in his own image. This God, who never existed before, even looks a bit like Archie.

The fact that he has the same skin color is revealed in an exchange between Archie and George Jefferson, the one and only time Archie's black neighbor comes to dinner.

Conversation between them is about as easy as between two persons who speak entirely different languages. The silence is broken by Archie, who believes that because his son-in-law Mike defends black people, they in turn must all think like Mike. Knowing Mike to be an atheist, Archie says to his guest, "You an atheist?"

George. No, I believe in God.

Archie. That's nice . . . Interestin', too! I mean how the black people went from worshipin' snakes and beads and wooden idols . . . all the way up to our God.

George. What do you mean, your God?

Archie. Well, he's the white man's God, ain't he?

George. That ain't necessarily so. What makes you think God isn't black?

Archie. Because God created man in his own image, and you'll note *I ain't black*.

George. Well, don't complain to me about it.

Archie. Look, you seen pictures of God, ain't ya? That Dago artist painted him on that ceiling in Rome . . . remember?

George. You mean that *white* Dago artist painted him.

Archie. Ev'ry picture I ever seen of God, he was white.

George. Maybe you were looking at the negatives.

Yes, maybe he has been looking at the negatives, but more likely Archie has been looking at too many pictures of himself.

This God who is white like Archie also has the same exclusive religion.

Archie. God made the world in seven days.

Edith. Six days, Archie.

Archie. Seven, Edith!

Edith. No. On the seventh day he rested.

Archie. Maybe half a day, but the other half he was checkin' on what he done . . .

"Everybody knows God is white."

Now this God-maker is going to rewrite the Bible.

Archie. . . . He made every one the same religion—Christians. Which he named after his Son, Christian . . . or Christ for short. And that's how it was for years. One religion. Until they started splitting 'em up into all them other denumerations. But there's still only one religion. His up there.

Mike. And of course that's the only one you belong to, Arch?

Archie. I'd be pretty stupid not to, wouldn't I?

Therefore everybody who does not accept Archie's God, who in this case creates the world in six and a half days and has a Son

"There's still only one religion. His up there."

named "Christian," or "Christ for short," is stupid. That may be pretty narrow, but it is handy, because Archie now has a fantastic tool for defending his own views—God. A good example of how he uses this instrument may be seen in the way he deals with progress.

Progress is hard for Archie, a battered victim of future shock, to handle. When he is confronted by the fearful and mysterious reality of organ transplants, he uses as a defense this God who thinks as he thinks.

Archie. When you gotta go, you gotta go. *(He intones this as if it were a Bible verse)* You go because *he* wants you. And when he wants you. And he don't want no quack doctors putting new hearts into you and keeping you here against his will, 'cause it throws him off his schedule. It throws him all off. Now you do that to him . . . throw his schedule off like that, and when you get up there, you'll have to answer to him, won't you? Because he'll want to know why you didn't come up when you were called. Why you were late. Why you ignored him.

How can Archie do this? How can he create a God no greater than his prejudices and fears, a God so inadequate and small?

If you were to ask him that question the answer would be simple, "It was easy." And Archie is not unique. Men and women have always created God in their own image. We all are tempted to reject the God of revelation and fashion a comfortable one.

The American has an American God. The hardhat a hardhat God. The executive an executive God. The militant a militant God. So when Archie creates an "Archie God," many people find this completely acceptable.

This Archie God is as nearsighted as his creator. He doesn't notice when his children hate, kill, cheat, lie, and destroy each other. It is belief in an unseeing God that allows Archie to refuse to give his old suit to a charity drive.

Archie. Listen, that's the trouble with this country—too many hand-outs. Today every bum and his brother is collecting welfare, which is just another way of picking my pocket. Well, if he's gonna pick my pocket, it ain't gonna be in *my* suit.

Because the theme song of this "cop-out God" is "Praise the Lord and Pass the Ammunition," Archie is able to speak of God and dropping "the Bomb" on "those pinko Commie Chinks" all in the same breath.

He takes pride in telling you that he never mixes religion and politics. Which makes his religion irrelevant for our kind of world and explains how he can be blind to corruption in his own political party; his God also overlooks "dirty tricks." It may seem preachy, but somehow it appears to me that the best thing this person could do would be to put some religion back into his politics.

The Archie God can be a great scapegoat. He is the one who gets blamed when Archie tries to duck responsibility. "It was the will of God." Archie, for instance, pompously justifies his lack of concern for the poor by intoning: "Jesus said, 'The poor you will always have with you.'" Jesus did say that. It is recorded in Matthew 26:11. But Archie reads it as a command to ignore poverty. It was not a command, but a rebuke to some insensitive disciples who complained about the wastefulness of the woman who anointed Jesus with expensive oil on the night before his crucifixion. Saying "the poor you will always have with you" was Jesus' way of predicting his imminent death, as

indeed he made clear, adding: "You will not always have me."
Strange how we followers of the "Alibi God" can cling to the
first half of this verse but fail to remember other words of Jesus,
as, "Go and sell all that you have and give it to the poor."

I am a little ambivalent about further attributes of the Archie
God because they are inconsistent. Sometimes Archie speaks of
him almost flippantly as "the Man Upstairs," while at other
times he casts him in an ecclesiastical mold suited to a resident
of church buildings only—this deity seems to enjoy hanging
around altars, getting his kicks out of hearing King James
English. His love of purple-passioned prayers is the reason
many of his nonclerical followers leave praying to the clergy.

Such a God is not only a little spooky, but to many seems
literally out of this world. He is impersonal, preventing his
followers from relating to him in the way they so desperately
need, as a child to a loving Parent, or a friend to a Friend who
really cares about them and their lives.

Archie's "God" is a counterfeit, and he must die so that Archie and all of us who are in so many ways like him can begin
to know the God of revelation. The One who is for us, not
against us; who takes pleasure in the joy of *all* his children and
wants us to live and laugh and love together.

When that "God" dies, we who have wrongfully created him
in our own image can be recreated by him in his image.

2

"Edith the Good"

What I like best about Archie is his wife Edith. I love Edith. At first I wrote her off in the same way Archie did, accepting his dehumanizing name for her, "Dingbat." Whatever that is, she is not a dingbat. She is an honest woman who, because she is in touch with herself, will admit that most of life is as frustrating as her experience of menopause.

Edith. I was just thinking, when I was a young girl, I never knew what every young girl was supposed to know. And now I'm gonna be an old lady, I don't know what every old lady is supposed to know.

This doesn't mean, however, that life has passed her by. Edith not only holds the world record for playing the "Minute Waltz" on the piano in seven and a half minutes, but also considers it some kind of record that she once kissed a boy nonstop for eleven and a half minutes. She still feels they could have gone fifteen had it not been for the fact that the boy had a buck tooth which gave her a shooting pain "from my upper lip to my right temple."

Edith is definitely not the smartest person you will ever meet. She thinks cocaine is one of the new diet drinks and wonders why the sandman is not Arab rather than Japanese, since Arabs have so much more sand. She makes donations to the Black Panthers because she wants to help save our wildlife. The main sources of her education seem to have been *Photoplay Magazine* and television. Having an affinity for medicine, she gives credit for her vast medical knowledge to Dr. Marcus Welby, though she is concerned that he has never had a show dealing with "the heartbreak of psoriasis."

In spite of her seeming naïvete and lack of education, there is something very special about Edith that draws you to her. Though we see it through the tunnel of her naïvete, it illuminates the world around her.

When Archie denounces Mike's idea of admitting the Red Chinese to the United Nations, Edith responds with the light of tolerance.

Archie. Never! This country ain't gonna sit down with a nation of Chink ping-pong players who don't believe in God!
Edith. God believes in them.

Her honesty shines a little too brightly in Archie's eyes when she explains how her shopping basket full of special-sale canned peaches broke away on the supermarket parking lot, ran downhill, and smashed into a parked car.

Archie. What did the owner of the car have to say?
Edith. Nothing. Nobody was there.

Archie. Nobody was there . . . Then you're in the clear! After all that rigamarole, wherein a man could have ten heart attacks, we find that she's absolutely in the clear.

Edith. Archie, I'm glad you're not mad.

Mike. He's not mad 'cause he got away with something! So what if another guy's car is damaged, Archie Bunker saved thirty bucks!

Archie. In a pig's sty, thirty bucks! They charge you that much for driving in to their garages. I'm just glad he don't know who done it!

Edith. Oh, he knows who done it!

Archie. Huh??

Edith. Well, I had to leave a note on the car to tell him how sorry I was and . . .

Archie. Edith! You left your name on that man's car!!

Edith. Yeah, with my address and phone number.

Archie. I don't believe it! I don't believe it! . . .

Mike. . . . That kind of honesty is rare these days.

Archie. Sure it's rare! An' you wanna know why? 'Cause there's about fourteen million people to every dingbat in this country . . . that's why it's rare!

Edith. Archie, you wouldn't want a stranger to pay for the damage that *I* caused, would ya?

Her sense of justice and personal integrity cannot be dimmed even when it must shine alone, as when she does jury duty. All the pressure from other jurors does not budge her from what she thinks is right. Archie knows immediately who the "lone juror" is when he sees the newspaper account.

Archie. (Reading aloud) "The jury in the Martinez trial was sent back to continue deliberations today after the judge refused to accept a split decision. It is understood that one lone juror is blocking a unanimous verdict." Lone juror, huh? They should have made it "Lone Dingbat."

Her understanding penetrates our moral darkness, and for this reason Edith is the "Christ figure" in most of the episodes. Not only does she stand for what is good and right, but she is the humble lamb who goes to slaughter again and again. Yet, even as from his agonizing death on the cross came the victory of resurrection, so out of Edith's seemingly constant small defeats come victories.

Typical is the episode in which Archie, Edith, Mike, and Gloria come home from a movie to find their house being robbed and the two intruders still at the scene. The burglars, who are black, immediately recognize that Archie is a bigot. He denies it. "Look, Archie Bunker ain't no bigot! I'm the the first to say—it ain't your fault you're colored!"

Mike is tagged too when one of the men exclaims, "Lordy me, we got a bigot and a liberal!"

They cannot label Edith so quickly, but neither can they ignore her. Somehow she is able to reach through the curtains of hostility, hurt, and hate to answer something in them which hasn't been touched for a long time. At their request she sings a corny little song she has written for a contest. One of them comments, "Oh man . . . that is one bad song! That must be the worst song I think I ever heard." But they respond differently to the unselfconscious, sincere woman who sings it; they are so moved that they find themselves unable to steal from her. Despite the faint cure in the program at times of both fantasy and farce, this rings true. The spokesman tries to explain it to Archie.

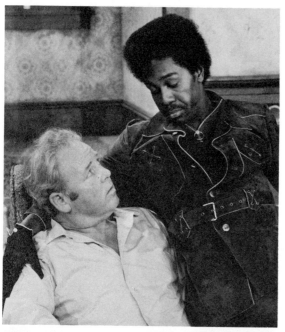

"A gen-u-wine *bigot.*"

"A gen-u-wine *liberal.*"

Burglar. I'll tell you something, old man. I got a problem. Now an' then I meet people . . . I mean, real people—like your wife here —and it's tough to steal from people. How could I take away *her* toaster . . . and *her* mixer . . . and *her* television?

They recognize her for what she is, neither a bigot, nor a liberal, nor a dingbat, but "people."

It is great to be people, to be human like Edith, but Archie doesn't understand it. He is turned around on what true humanity is, as appears when he discovers that in their card games all these years she has been letting him win. He blows his top.

Archie. That's you all right, Edith the Good. You'll stoop to anything to be good. You never yell. You never swear. You never make nobody mad. You think it's easy living with a saint? Even when you cheat you don't cheat to win. You cheat to lose. Edit', you ain't human.

Edith. That's a terrible thing to say, Archie Bunker. I am just as human as you are.

Archie. Oh yeah . . . then prove you're just as human as me. Do something rotten.

He thinks it is only human to kill, to hate, and whatever else "rotten" might include. But these things are *inhuman*, it is our inhumanity that is the problem. We need to become human like Edith.

When Jesus preached the Sermon on the Mount one of the things he said was, "Blessed are the meek for they shall inherit the earth." That always sounded unbelievable to me. The meek? Inherit the earth?

"Edith the Good"

Edith helps me to understand. She is obviously one of the "blessed meek" who will inherit after all of us Archie types have died of the many stress diseases that result from our ambition and our pride.

Praise God for Edith the Meek, Edith the Good. She and her kind are our hope. But I believe she is also Archie's hope in a very special way. Someday she is going to kiss that old frog, and he is going to turn into a handsome prince.

3

God's Kind of Atheist

Assume you have never heard of Archie Bunker or his son-in-law Mike before. You don't know who believes in God and who is the atheist.

On violence:

Mike. Violence won't help!
Archie. What's wrong with revenge? That's a perfect way to get even.

On capital punishment:

Archie. Anybody who goes around bothering other people, the only decent thing to do is knock 'em off. If you can't do it yourself, bring back the old death penalty.
Mike. Arch, I don't believe what I'm hearing. That just makes murderers of us all. I don't want to murder anyone and I don't want the state murdering in my name.

"You are a meathead!"

When Edith wants to use the family savings to publish a song she has written, Archie denies her because he wants to use the money to buy a gun.

Mike. Once again, when it's a question of guns or butter—books or bombs—when it's a question of destructive man or creative man —creative man gets the shaft.

Mike is concerned about pollution. Archie couldn't care less.

Mike continually affirms Edith's honesty; Archie sees it as stupidity.

Mike sees people as Blacks, Vietnamese, and Jewish. Archie sees them as Jungle Bunnies, Gooks, and Kikes.

Now which is the atheist? Believe it or not, it is the nonviolent, concerned-about-others, sensitive, and loving Mike. The violent, self-centered, bigoted, dishonest dehumanizer is the believer. No wonder Mike doesn't believe in God.

I would like to tell Mike that the God revealed in the Bible and through Jesus has many of the same concerns as himself. For Mike has a warmth and sensitivity which I should think might cause him to respond very positively to the real God, if Archie's version would just get out of the way. Since it is hard for Mike intellectually to accept God, I would like him to consider some of the traditional "proofs" of God as I understand them.

The Pool Ball Proof. Imagine time as a great pool table, and from our end of the table we see a ball come rolling into the pocket. Where did it get its momentum and direction? It was hit by another ball, which was hit by another, which was hit by another, which was hit by another, and so on all the way back to the ball that was hit by a cue stick guided and pushed by someone. That someone, whom philosophers call the Unmoved Mover, others call God.

The Watchmaker Proof. Philosophers call this the "argument from design." One of them explains it by a parable about a man who stumbles upon a watch, something he has heard of but never seen before. He studies it closely to observe its shape, design, mechanism, its movement and ability to keep time. What does he say? "By accident all these parts came together

"God's kind of atheist."

in this way. By chance they move, and by chance they keep time." No. He says, "I've found a watch—somewhere there must be a watchmaker."

When I look at the universe, there is an order more accurate than any watch in its tides and seasons and orbits, its molecules and light years. Do I say "by chance"? No. Rather, "I have found a universe—somewhere there must be a Universe-Maker."

The Ought Proof. The very fact that we have the word *ought* in our vocabulary is a proof of God to some of us. This has been traditionally called the moral argument. There seems to be a universal sense of right, of what "ought" to be in the heart of every person. That sense in itself is common to all law codes despite enormous cultural differences.

The "Reaching-Up" Proof. Anthropologists say there has never been a known tribe of people which did not practice some form of prayer. The human being is a praying animal. We seem to know instinctively that there is Someone greater toward whom we long and yearn. There is Something toward which we turn in the same way a flower reaches for the sun or a compass points north. That something many call God.

These are just some of the perennial "proofs" for God's existence. Having explored a few of them, I must admit they would not have much effect on Mike. And I am glad, for the business of trying to prove God is a rather silly game. Any serious attempt shrinks God down to the limits of our finite minds. And Mike's atheism may not be an intellectual conclusion anyway. Believing in God is more a matter of will or experience than of the mind. It is fundamentally with our wills, against a sketchy background of experience to give us reasons, that we decide to believe or not to believe. We often then adjust our reasons to support our decision.

The biggest obstacle to Mike's believing, I am convinced, is the example of those who call themselves believers. When Archie asks, "What have you got against God?" Mike confesses, "Nothing. Can't you understand that, Archie? I don't have anything against God or the notion of God. It is what people do in his name that I don't like. They hate in his name. They kill in his name."

Mike does not stand alone. Quite a number of people react the same way, and their response is understandable. But there is the other side of the coin. Some pretty exciting things have been done in God's name. There are those who have loved in his name, healed in his name, taught in his name, and sacrificed in his name. For every Archie there is an Albert Schweitzer or a David Livingston or a Joe Smoe who takes the business of loving his neighbor seriously.

Then there is one special Man who was called Emmanuel, "God With Us," and he is one through whom I believe Mike could make an authentic discovery of God. Mike's protests against violence, capital punishment, guns, injustice, and bigotry show that he is a person of high ideals. This "God With Us" (others call him Jesus) fleshes out these ideals beyond our wildest expectations. He took on the mighty and raised up the weak. He was so responsive to ordinary things of life that when a wedding party was in danger of embarrassment because the supply of wine ran out, he provided more wine so that the couple might continue their celebration with their friends.

Better still, he changed persons. He could take a self-centered religious bigot and change him into a tender, caring human being named Paul.

He could take a stingy little crook, Zacchaeus, and change him into an abundant giver.

He changed an unnamed Samaritan whore into an evangelist for his cause.

He could raise the dead.

That was two thousand years ago. But there are some who, believing he is still with us, have bet their lives on him so that he can continue his life-changing caring through us. He inspires us, empowers us, and leads us to share the Good News of life that is available to all.

You would like him, Mike!

4

Gloria, Working for First-Class Citizenship

Like most of us, Gloria is a person struggling for her identity. As with more than half of us, the struggle is complicated by the fact that she is a woman in a society which too often treats women as second-class citizens. Gloria is not willing to settle for this status for herself or any other woman, including her mother. In fact, it is in defense of Edith that Gloria makes her emancipation proclamation.

Edith is trying to show some creativity by changing the monotonous Sunday breakfast of "eggs over easy and crisp bacon" to a special soufflé of which she is very proud. Archie is not impressed, and won't even taste the soufflé.

Gloria. Wow! A woman sure has no chance to express herself around you. It's as if she were in prison. She can't grow, she can't change, she's second-class, half a person. . . . Women are individuals—*your* wife is an individual! And she's entitled to the same rights and privileges as you!

"Women have some rights, too."

Gloria's words must be heard. All of us who would cause any human being to have the kinds of feelings she describes must face our own bigotry, as Archie must face up to his, and change.

Archie face up to his bigotry and change? Is that possible? Yes, and Paul, the bigot from Tarsus (later known as St. Paul), is a perfect illustration of the possibility. At one time, each day he used to recite this prayer:

> Praises be to God that thou has not created me to be a Gentile.
> Praises be to God that thou has not created me to be a woman.

Praises be to God that thou hast not created me to be an
ignorant man.

But Paul changed, for he later (in Galatians 3:28) wrote a statement of emancipation which gave evidence of a complete turn-
about.

> There is neither Jew nor Greek,
> There is neither slave nor free,
> There is neither male nor female.
> For you are all one in Christ Jesus.

The person and message of Jesus Christ changed Paul drasti-
cally. The main thrust of the ministry of Jesus was liberation,
and that was what Paul committed himself to.

It is clear that there was a steady insistence by Jesus on a
rightful valuing of women and respect for their individuality.
This may be hard for some to believe, considering that woman
has historically too often been the "nigger" of the Church.
Nevertheless, the biblical record shows that Jesus displayed a
quiet concern to affirm the value of women.

In a day when others were praying, like Paul before his con-
version, "Praises be . . . that thou has not created me a woman,"
Jesus had women among his traveling companions, along with
the twelve disciples. This was of such significance that Luke
points it out in verses 2 and 3 of the eighth chapter of his Gospel.

A more significant break with tradition came when Jesus
compared himself, as well as God and the hosts of heaven, with
a woman in the parable of the Woman and the Lost Coin (Luke
15:8–9).

Jesus' tranquil assumption of the equality of women was hard
to accept, for those who had been conditioned otherwise—even
many women. He rebukes one of his best friends, Martha, when
she protests her sister Mary's taking what was then a man's role

by sitting "at the Lord's feet and listening to his teaching" (Luke 10:39–42), rather than fulfilling the traditional feminine duty of serving.

Other examples of Jesus' view of women could be given. Being a person of profound insight, he must have known how incredibly important his first appearance after the resurrection would be for his followers and for all the world. To whom would he appear—to the high priests at the Temple or the local Walter Cronkite? He chose a woman, and we must never forget it (John 20:11–18).

Mary stood weeping outside the tomb. Still crying, she bent over to look into it and saw two angels dressed in white sitting where the body of Jesus had lain. "Woman, why are you crying?" they asked her. She answered, "They have taken my Lord away, and I do not know where they have put him!" And she turned around and saw Jesus standing there; her eyes perhaps blurred with tears, she did not know it was he.

"Woman, why are you crying?" he asked. "Whom do you seek?" She thought he was the gardener, and begged him, "If you have moved him, sir, tell me where you have put him, and I will take him away." Then Jesus said to her, "Mary!" and she turned toward him and said in Hebrew, "Rabboni!" which means "Teacher."

"Do not cling to me," Jesus told her, "for I have not yet gone back up to the Father. But go to my brothers and tell them for me, 'I go back up to him who is my Father and your Father, my God and your God.' " So Mary Magdalene told the disciples that she had seen the Lord, and what he had said to her.

Jesus sees women Gloria's way. But what about Archie, who interprets the Bible differently? "The Bible says God made man in his image. Then he made woman from a rib—a cheap cut."

Can Archie change? He probably won't be able to alter his attitude toward women until he works out his own understanding of masculinity. His ideas are leftovers from the age of the dinosaurs, or Alley Oop comic strips. Unfortunately not extinct by a long sight.

"Moose" Hansen is Archie's ideal man. He is "the most respected guy in the whole Bowlin' League."

Mike. What makes him so respected?

Archie. What makes him so respected! Well, I'll give you a for instance! One day he's standin' out in front of the bowlin' alley arguing with some jerk over politics or something, and this jerk makes his final remark and he thinks he has Moose put away. You know what Moose done?

Mike. What?

Archie. He went over and ripped the door off the guy's car.

Mike. An intelligent man.

Archie. You're damn right. Then another time in the bowling alley he was waiting to get the phone to call his wife. And there was this hippy weirdo on the phone, so Moose started tapping on the door but the weirdo won't get off. So finally, do you know what Moose did?

Mike. He ripped the door off the phone booth.

Archie. I told you the story before.

For Archie a true man is a moose, an animal. Such a standard not only makes him feel personally inadequate but also disgusts him with Michael, whose tenderness, empathy, and artistic taste he rejects as "feminine."

Ironically, on the same day that Archie and Mike talked about Moose, Gloria bought Mike a present of a new leather shoulder

"Gloria, bride and woman."

pouch. This, which Archie insists on calling a purse, so threatens
his stereotype of a real man that he asks Gloria why she didn't

buy Mike a matching pair of panty hose.

How do we discern the true "man" here? Which of the two is it? I would have to answer that question on the basis of how they relate to their wives.

Archie's treatment of his wife is condensed into two words. He consistently says to her: "Stifle yourself!" Whenever Edith tries to speak up, show any individuality, or do anything that does not fit the mold he has made for her, his response is "Stifle yourself!" Yet he has a deep affection for her, as we see in glimpses here and there; and also when they retrace the steps of their honeymoon. It's like pulling teeth, but he does very occasionally—awkwardly—admit his real feeling.

Mike on the other hand, despite recurrent unthinking relapses into old patterns of behavior, is able to say to his wife, "I love you. And I need you and I know how much. In here," (pointing to his heart) "alone, we need each other, each one as much as the other. We're equal—totally equal."

It takes a human being who is pretty secure in his own masculinity to be able to say what Mike says. A fearful person finds it necessary to put down members of the opposite sex by claiming some kind of sexual superiority. The true liberation of women will happen when men are liberated from some of the leftover caveman concepts of masculinity.

5

Archie and Adam

Getting to know Archie has been, to say the least, a baffling experience for me. Our relationship is a real love-hate thing. The first time I saw him I found myself reacting to him as my enemy; I disliked nearly everything about him. I couldn't stand his self-righteousness.

Edith. I was just thinking. In all the years we been married, you never once said you was sorry.

Archie. Edith, I'll gladly say that I'm sorry—if I ever do anything wrong.

Nor could I stand his bigotry, which he denies to George Jefferson, his black neighbor (as he does to the burglars), in such blandly appalling terms: ". . . I'm the first to say—it ain't your fault you're colored."

But as I have grown to know him, I have come to like him in spite of his weaknesses. Part of my liking comes from an empathy and understanding for Archie as a complex person. More significantly, he has helped me to understand myself. When I first met him I thought we were complete opposites. But more and more I am discovering that we have a good deal in common.

Another person who has helped me to understand myself is Adam. In fact, these two have also so much in common that for me, Archie *is* Adam. He is a cigar-smoking Adam with clothes on. Like me he is a fugitive from the Garden of Eden. The story of Adam can help us to understand both ourselves and Archie. In looking at it we may be comparing Adam and Archie, but let us not forget that there is much of Archie/Adam in each of us.

Adam (whose name means "Everyman") and his wife Eve lived in a park called Eden. Eden Park seems to have had everything a desert-living people would dream of, including an abundance of trees which provide shade as well as every variety of fruit.

All the fruit is for the pleasure of Adam and Eve except for that of one tree, which they are not to eat and which they do not touch until a serpent comes along with an exciting promise. If they eat the prohibited fruit, they will be like God. Knowing they will never get a better offer, and not realizing that the serpent is a liar, they eat the fruit.

Time passes and the scene ends with two bloated nudes sitting under an empty tree surrounded by a giant pile of apple cores.*

That desire to be like God led to their downfall, and to the downfall of all humanity since. A God is whatever is Number One in a person's life, and with Adam and Eve it was "self" that

---

*The Bible does not say it was an apple tree. I tend to guess it was most probably an olive tree, since I find I respond to olives and sin in much the same way, one small thing leading to another.

"A cigar-smoking Adam with clothes on."

received that first slot. It sounds pretty harmless until you look at mankind historically and realize that our "wanting to be like God," our me-first attitude, our concern for self-elevation, is the one common denominator in all the violence in our world. All the war, the hell in our families, the breakdowns in our personal relationships are started within the hearts of human beings who have self-elevation as their first priority in life. Thus Archie proclaims his creed to Mike:

Archie. I've been making my way in this world for a long time, sonny boy, and one thing I know—a man better watch out for number one. It's the survival of the fittess!

Very similar words could have come from Adam's mouth just before he bit into the fruit. Archie and Adam are both idolators, for the slot they both claim for themselves belongs to God.

Another way of understanding man's predicament is to think of life as a kingdom in which the basic question is who is going to be king—me or God? Gloria knows how Archie answers that question as she watches her mother bow to his commands.

Gloria. Submitting to him. That's what she's doing. Submitting to her king . . . her ruler . . . her lord and master.
Archie. Ain't that a nice way of putting it?

Archie likes the idea of ruling from his throne in the center of the living room, referred to by all as Archie's chair. He is threatened when he finds anyone else in it—especially George Jefferson. He orders Jefferson out of the chair, and when George refuses to move, threatens to call the cops. Why? Because this is a threat to his kingdom.

No wonder Jesus told us when we pray to pray, "Thy kingdom

"Archie enthroned."

come, thy will be done." Our commitment and our predicament is "my kingdom come, my will be done," and our only hope, as is Archie's, is to change the *my* to *thy*.

If we do not change the *my* where does it bring us? In Adam and Eve's story it leads to a strange kind of self-consciousness which the Bible describes: "Then the eyes of both were opened, and they knew they were naked; and they sewed fig leaves together and made themselves aprons."

An apron is all right if you don't have to turn around and don't mind going through life sideways with your back to the wall. Which pretty well describes Archie, who has a whole wardrobe of aprons, all used for the same reason: to hide the real Archie, to keep anyone from really knowing him.

His aprons have many different names—"knowledgeable," "strong," "patriotic." There is one that says "Don't touch me!"; another, "adequate." It is the "adequate" apron that Archie wears most often; and its very inadequacy is what makes him react so strongly when he discovers that Edith has been letting him win at Monopoly all the years of their married life.

Edith. Well, Archie, I thought it would make you feel better if I let you win.

Archie. Let me win? That'll be the day when I can't win without you letting me win. You spoiled the whole thing. From now on if you want to do something together, do it by yourself!

"Do it together by yourself?" Obviously you can't, just as you can't do most things by yourself. People need people, and whether Archie likes it or not he needs people too. The inscription on his adequacy apron that says "I don't need nobody" just isn't true. Yet he still tries to hide behind that and other coverings—which is his "perogatory," but he will never know life as it really is until he drops them.

Aprons isolate Archie from his true self, from others, and from God. That is why he holds everyone at arm's length by degrading them with such names as "pinko," "colored," "Kikes," "Wops," "Meathead," and "Dingbat." Nearly everyone is in some sense his enemy. He is left with his aprons, which imprison him, and his soul shrivels in that prison, which is becoming a tomb.

Is there any hope for Archie and the rest of us self-centered, apron-wearing, isolated humans?

The answer is Yes! In the Bible there is a story about another entombed man named Lazarus. He has been dead four days before Jesus arrives on the scene, mourns with Lazarus' sisters, and then goes to the tomb.

The scene is simple. Jesus asks some friends to remove the stone door from the tomb, which they do. Standing in front of the opening he calls, "Lazarus, come forth." And Lazarus emerges wrapped in burial cloths, which Jesus asks his friends to help remove.

He is alive. Released, like a butterfly from the cocoon, a blossom from the bud.

That is my dream for Archie and all of us—that we may respond to the enabling command of Jesus to "come forth" from our self-imposed prisons, freed from all that binds us and keeps us from being the whole persons God means us to be.

Once in a while Archie does open up just a little bit. When he wanted to get on the Cannonballers bowling team, he gave us a clue as to his real need.

Archie. Oh, Edith, I want to be on that team so bad I can taste it. And another thing. You should see the bowling shirts them Cannonballers got. All yellow silk, with bright red piping on the collar and the sleeves.

Edith. And you look so good in yellow.

Archie. Yeah, I look good in yellow. And on the back there's a picture of a cannon firing a bowling ball at a set of pins. Beautiful. When you got something like that on your back, Edith, you know you're somebody.

"Know you're somebody"—that's what Archie wants. He wants to be somebody. The amazing thing is that if he would ever stop wearing those aprons and come out of that tomb, he would discover what I am discovering whenever I get a peek behind his unconsciously shy, even timid cover-up. There is a great human being hidden there. He *is* somebody.

Archie, come forth!

6

Archie and the Prodigal Son

Sometimes I fantasize what would happen if Archie came to my study for counseling. People come every day, and—unlikely as it may sound—I see no reason why he might not, like them, reach the point where he recognizes that life has not lived up to its billing—is not all that he had hoped and anticipated.

What would I say to Archie if he did come? My first thought is that I would tell him about the crucifixion of Jesus and the meaning that event has for our lives. But when I consider how his desire to be number one and his drive for isolation have affected his eyesight, I realize he probably cannot see the crucifixion for what it is. His bigotry probably causes him to see "Jews killing his boy" rather than seeing the death of Christ as the supreme demonstration of God's love.

No, I think Archie would be helped most if we could talk about some of the truths to be found in the story told by Jesus concerning a Prodigal Son.

The little story is a classic, not only because of its simplicity but because we all are in it.

"Life is not all he had hoped it would be."

It is about a father who had two sons. "And the younger of them said to his father, 'Father, give me the share of property that falls to me.' And he divided his living between them. Not many days later the younger son gathered all he had and took his journey into a far country. . . ." There the boy squandered his property and spent everything, and when a great famine occurred he began to be in need, so he went to work for a man who sent him into the fields to feed pigs. He envied them their food, for he was hungry, and no one gave him anything. Finally he came to himself and realized that even his father's servants were better off. And he determined to go back to his father and make a clean breast of it. "Father [he planned to say], I have sinned against heaven and before you; I am no longer worthy to be called your son; treat me as one of your hired servants." So he went home.

And we read in the account:

But while he was yet at a distance, his father saw him and had compassion, and ran and embraced him and kissed him. And the son said to him, "Father, I have sinned against heaven and before you; I am no longer worthy to be called your son." But the father said to his servants, "Bring quickly the best robe, and put it on him; and put a ring on his hand, and shoes on his feet; and bring the fatted calf and kill it, and let us eat and make merry; for this my son was dead, and is alive again; he was lost, and is found." And they began to make merry. (Luke 15:20–24 RSV)

Meanwhile the older brother, coming in from the fields, heard music and dancing and asked what it was. When he knew the reason for it he was angry and would not go in. His father came and tried to persuade him, but he complained that for years he had been a good son yet had never been given even a kid, to feast with his friends. But when his wastrel brother came—"who has devoured your living with harlots"—it was another matter. And the father said to him, in the classic reply of Jesus' story, "Son, you are always with me, and all that is mine is yours. It was fitting to make merry and be glad, for this your brother was dead, and is alive; he was lost, and is found."

Now I can envision Archie reacting to a number of things here. He reacts especially to the younger son, who represents a lot of mankind, be it the "Midnight Cowboy," or the country bumpkin who goes to find out if everything really is up to date in Kansas City, or the spoiled rich boy who gets wiped out in Las Vegas. For Archie you don't have to take a journey to reach the "far country." You can arrive merely by changing your appearance, like the long-haired visitor who came to the Bunker front door.

Mike. You remember Paul Goodnow from Boston. He was my best man at the wedding.
Archie. Oh, yeah. I remember *him*. Who's this?
Mike. That's him.
Archie. You? You're that nice kid with the neat hair and the nice suit . . . ?

Gloria. Paul is not weird! Because, you used to *like* him.
Archie. I liked him when he was a clean-cut engineering student who wanted to build bridges and banks. Now he looks like somebody who wants to blow them up.

This feeling about Paul is the same kind of response Archie would probably have to the younger son, who he would think shouldn't have received a share of the property in the first place. The fact that the boy ends up with the pigs is only a "just award."

Archie could not, one suspects, identify with the younger son. He would have little pity or understanding for him. Yet you can't help but think that Archie, too, must surely at some time or other have had the desire to go his own way, to find fulfillment by doing his own thing. He too must have seen the billboards and heard enticing claims for the far country, all promising the abundant life. Surely he has been tempted to believe that big lie—?

If he has, he is not ready to admit it. He is not willing to identify with the "prodigal," whom he sees not so much as a person but as another generation which has contaminated the faith.

Archie. Jesus Christ, Superstar! Your whole damn generation—we try to talk sense to ya,—we take you to church—we teach you religion—and you give us back the Son of God like he's some "Englebum Hunkerdunk."

It is ironic that Archie reacts so negatively, for the place where the young Prodigal finally ends up is where Archie craves to be: enjoying the "good life" of a party, the fatted calf, music, dancing, and friends.

That quality of life became a reality for the Prodigal when he "came to himself" and headed back home a changed person, who now says not "give *me* what is *mine*" but "make me *your* servant." Though the connection may seem obscure, in reality that change started the party going, and the same can happen for any person who will make the same turnaround.

Archie would also reject the father in the story. I can hear him say, "What's wrong with that guy? He's one of them permissive daddies, letting the kid take off with all that money and then sperlin' him with a party when he crawls back with his tail between his legs."

Obviously, Archie would find it hard to understand that the father in the story represents God. It would be interesting to tell him only the first part of the tale, stop in the middle where the Prodigal Son is returning home, and ask him what he thinks the the father would or should do.

Archie might be more impressed with the father in a similar

story in Buddhist literature, who acts with caution, hiding from the son and putting him through a series of tests until he is assured of the genuineness of his reformation.

Then there is the "You've had your chance" type of father (God), condemning the boy to hell; or the "Let's make a deal" type who says, "You can come back, provided _____ and _____." (Let the reader fill in the blanks—the requirement possibilities are infinite, from going to church every Sunday to taking a vow of celibacy.)

Archie could probably accept either of these types of God, or perhaps a divine Cheerleader who would stay on the porch shouting his verbal support: "C'mon boy, you can do it! Pull up your socks, think positive!" But the God symbolized by the father of the Prodigal Son is baffling to him.

What the father did in Jesus' story would seem to Archie embarrassing and degrading. For that father was overcome with love's impatience. Seeing his son appear on the road, he sprang from the porch, ran to meet "the dirty little good-for-nothing," and threw his arms around him. Before the boy could fully utter his confession he was reinstated as a son. The party was planned, the calf was killed, and all his friends were invited in to celebrate.

If only Archie could believe in a Father/God like that rather than the kind he talks to in the middle of an argument with Mike—

Mike. Arch, there is no heaven, there is no hell and there is no God.
Archie. There he goes again, God! Did you hear that, Lord?
Mike. Oh, Arch . . . **(Begins choking on food and sputtering)**
Gloria. Michael, What's the matter?
Mike. (Still choking) Food . . . went . . . down . . . wrong way.

Archie. That's God payin' him back. Shovin' them words down your throat.

Gloria. (Pounding him on the back) Raise your arms over your head, honey!

Archie. The hell with him. Let him struggle. Serves you right, Meathead! Nobody fools around with the Lord . . . Go get him, God! Give it to him good, God! Do your stuff, Lord.

Choking people to death? That is not "his stuff"—"his stuff" is forgiveness, love, and celebration.

7

The Elder Brother

While Archie, like most of us, has more in common with the
Prodigal Son than he is willing to admit, there is a sense in
which he would be right in saying, "I ain't no Prodigal." He is
much more like the elder brother.

This was a "good boy" who stayed home. He was probably
correct when he complained to his father, "Lo, these many
years I have served you, and I never disobeyed your command." I am sure Archie sees himself in much the same way.
He has never broken the law, in his own mind he has been
responsible, he goes to work every day and brings home a
weekly paycheck. He is no runaway from the humdrum scene.

But the similarity goes deeper. He seems to share the unblessed feeling that expresses itself in the elder brother's words
to his father, "You never gave me a kid that I might make merry
with my friends." The Mom-always-liked-you-the-best feeling.

In the parable the older brother is left outside the party
looking in. The feeling he must have, coupled with that of
not being blessed, is also expressed by Archie in much that he

says and does. When Gloria talks about human rights he responds:

Archie. What about my rights? I know I got a lot going against me. I'm white, I'm Protestant and I'm hardworking—but can't you find some lousy amendment that protects me?

He sees himself as the eternal victim, whether because of big business—

Archie. Insurance companies live to cancel out guys like me.

or because of Edith—

Archie. Edith, why don't you just buy me a gun I can shoot myself with? It won't be so messy. I just cut myself four times in three seconds. Pieces of my face is down the drain on the way to the ocean. One of these days I will probably de-head myself. For the last time . . . *don't use my razor!*

What happens to people who feel unblessed, left out, and victimized? For one thing, they become bitter and judgmental.

Archie. If society is at fault that we got killers running around murdering innocent people, then its simple. We turn the killer loose, give him a pension for life and shoot the rest of the city.

That's why it is scary to think what would have happened if the older brother had been on the front porch rather than the father when the Prodigal returned. I am sure the latter would have seriously considered going back to the pigs rather than put up with the pietistic smugness with which his brother would have greeted him.

The effect the self-righteous have on others is bad enough, but what they do to themselves is worse. They actually become spiritual cripples who are unable to enjoy life to the full. We get a glimpse of this in the inability of the older brother to accept his father's urging to come in to the party and enjoy the friends and music and dancing.

Archie has been disabled in the same way. He is allergic to parties, joy, and hilarity. His attitude at Christmas is a good example.

Archie. Stifle, Edith. Let's have a little Silent Night around here for a change . . . I'm the only one around here thinking of the real solemn meaning of Christmas. Which is supposed to be a time of peace and quiet contemplation.

Edith. But I think you're allowed to be jolly too.

Archie. Sure, Edith, I never said you shouldn't be jolly. Just be jolly with your mouth shut.

Archie doesn't smile a lot, and he often gets upset when his family has something to smile about.

Archie. Well, when Gloria smiles with them straight teeth showing, I think of the three hundred and eighteen bucks it cost for the braces. When Edith smiles the same way, I think its gotta be gas. As for Mike, I think his underwear's too tight.

Is there any medicine for spiritual cripples? Yes there is! You can get well by accepting the father's invitation to the party, and I'm going to suggest a further remedy. Archie needs to learn how to dance. How Edith would love that! She knows Archie needs to be loosened up.

Edith. The other day I came across our copy of Glenn Miller's "Moonlight Serenade." You remember how we used to dance to that? Remember how I used to snuggle up against your cheek?
Archie. Oh, c'mon—will ya act your age? Even Fred Astaire and Ginger Rogers don't dance together no more.

Edith has the answer, Archie. We need to learn how to dance again. God's people need to choose dancing as their style of life. King David danced before the Ark of the Covenant in the Old Testament. Tyndale in the prologue to his translation of the New Testament in 1525 said, "The Gospel makes man's heart glad and makes him sing, dance, and leap for joy."

In our day there is much that God's people have to communicate that words just plain cannot handle. But our dancing style can; it can communicate joy and the abundant life. Let's build a whole repertoire of dances.

To begin with, let's do a sort of free dance where you just catch the rhythm of the universe. For too long we have been living by the numbers, in blocks of time taking our spiritual steps like some kind of Frankenstein's monster. But in the universe there is a swing to God's rhythm. Let's be a part of that rhythm.

Let's also follow that great dancer whom for a long time I didn't even consider to be a dancer: Charlie Chaplin. His very walk is a dance. He goes through life doing a dance step. Things are falling down all around him, the world is literally going to hell. That doesn't stop him, he just keeps on moving—keeps on dancing. Let's learn to dance like that.

"Edith the dancer."

Let's have such an assurance of the Lordship of Jesus Christ and the fact that he holds the future in his hands that, in spite of what may look like hopeless times, we can continue to dance on to our destination.

There are wrestlers who dance. There are hockey players who dance. The performance of an athlete full of the exuberance and grace of his own specialty can teach us a lot.

The dancing I have most enjoyed watching was in a movie some years ago called *Seven Brides for Seven Brothers.* I have never seen such dancers. They were enthusiastic, risky, and exciting. There was obvious danger involved in the kind of dancing they were doing, which was overcome by a real air of abandon.

I want to dance with a crowd that can dance like that. We have all been to enough stuffy church meetings, with their reticent resolutions that water down the gospel's demands and play it safe. Let's risk something for the sake of Jesus Christ and do it with a new kind of enthusiasm and excitement.

What would happen to Edith, Gloria, and Mike if some night when Archie came home from work he came in dancing? It would change their lives.

Could Archie and the rest of us really change that much? We certainly could. All we have to do is to hear, believe, and respond to the words of the Father to the older brother: "Son you are always with me, and all that is mine is yours. Come on in to the party."

"Come to the party, Archie."

8

Archie and Death

"Everybody's gotta die sometime. That's life," is Archie's response to a rebuke by Gloria for being so gleeful over the death
of a player on the bowling team. Archie is next in line for
membership on the team. But don't let his remark persuade
you to think that he is especially brave when it comes to dealing
with death. When his peripatetic cousin Oscar dies while visit-
ing the Bunkers, Archie crumbles, and it is Edith who proves
adequate to the situation.

She is not half so brave however as those who produced that
"All in the Family" episode entitled "The Saga of Cousin Oscar." Ironically, in a society in which we talk more and more
about sex, we have been talking less and less about human
mortality. We have pulled a reverse on the Victorians by
switching the taboo from sex to death. "All in the Family" met
the subject head-on, revealing that when an area of human
experience becomes taboo, we ourselves become victims of our
own ignorance.

The program introduces us to a new character in the Bunker

"Everybody's gotta die sometime. That's life."

neighborhood, Whitehead the undertaker. The script writers describe him as "a neighborhood funeral director. Decked out for his job in proper garb and prose, Whitehead is nonetheless a product of Queens."

Edith describes him more simply as a "mortician who talks like a Mother's Day card." Though he is not to be confused with all funeral directors, neither should he be written off as unreal. He personifies much of what is wrong in our attitude toward death. Whitehead is first of all a salesman, and we can recognize in his sales pitch some of the fallacies in our beliefs and customs relating to death.

He begins this way:

Ya see, our main interest at Whitehead Brothers is this: first and foremost, we want to create a beautiful and lastin' memory pitcher of the loved one.

Who is he kidding? A dead loved one in a casket is not beautiful no matter how extensive the makeup or expensive the casket. It is the life the person lived that can create "beautiful and lastin' memories." For my part, I want my family to remember me as I lived, and if I am unable to contribute anything in my lifetime, I doubt that my dead body will do any better.

Whitehead continues his sales pitch by showing a picture of a casket which sounds made to order for Archie.

Here is our 3292, Arch. The motif is Early American, as you see, maple hardwood, red, white, and blue quilting . . . and painted on the inside lid . . . the American Flag.

(A more recent model has "Peace with Honor" inscribed on the lid.)

Archie, whose ambivalence about death is expressed by the fact that he has put on a tie, the ultimate sacrifice, begins to warm to the "patriotic even in death" concept and asks the price of such a box. His terminology is immediately corrected by Whitehead: "The *casket*, Arch—his home for eternity."

In referring to the casket in this manner, Whitehead expresses one of four currently prevailing views of death. One is that man is like a clock which has been wound up only to run down and be placed in a grave forever. To Job's question, "If a man die shall he live again?" this concept answers a simple No. For some of us that is not acceptable, for something in us says that the God who takes such pains to create man—the crown of his creation—would not make us for only three score years and ten.

There are certain extensions of this outlook toward an idea of immortality. A second view dwells on the notion that our posterity is our life eternal. But is that life? Isn't it just a tune whistled in the dark? What about the person who has no descendants? Many do not.

A third view suggests that our life continues as we are remembered by others. Adherents to this emphasis like to use the example of Abraham Lincoln as he lives in our memories. Again we must wonder to ourselves: "That's living?" But more concretely, we are not all Abraham Lincolns. Most persons are not remembered for very long—few if any for eternity, while some die nameless, many without younger surviving relationships.

A rather different view of our status after death, which seems to be growing in popularity, is that of reincarnation: we die to be born again in another earthly life. In some versions this involves coming back higher or lower in the scale of creation than we are at present. If you are good you may return as a Mahatma Gandhi, or if you are very bad, as a horned toad or a slug. In (to us) more natural-sounding forms of this theory, we simply take on one human life after another, gradually correcting our weaknesses of character by long experience and moving toward a perfection envisioned in various ways.

I admit I am oversimplifying, but the first form of this idea raises some weird questions. Should I slap that mosquito who may be my grandfather? Such a decision must be based on the morality of the mosquito. If he is a bad mosquito, don't slap him, for he will be degraded in his next life. But if he is a good mosquito, go ahead. Who knows—maybe he'll come back as a lightning bug.

This is not really meant to be frivolous, though it may suggest insensitiveness to philosophies that have a deep reverence for all forms of life. These remarks are just a rather light way of recognizing the difficulties. But even the mildest idea of reincarnation, by its obliteration of memory, cuts squarely across what we think of as personal life or identity. For me, the contemporary song writer says it well, "I've Gotta Be Me." God calls us to be unique persons for eternity. Reincarnation would seem to deny us the privilege of fulfilling that calling.

All these concepts are considered by their holders as positive views of death. Scripture, on the contrary, takes a negative view. It sees death as the enemy, "the *last* enemy to be destroyed," says the Apostle Paul. It is God's response to death that gives us hope. The Bible speaks of the "resurrection body," which is a pretty hard idea to grasp. Jesus makes the analogy of a kernel of grain falling into the earth. Paul points out that the implanted seed is very different than the "body" of the full-grown wheat, even though there is still a relationship between the seed which is buried in the ground, and the full-grown wheat which lives.

Such a concept assures me that I will not be some kind of

spook or ghost in the hereafter, but will know a kind of wholeness that can only be understood in the context of a resurrection
body, and that I will not lose my uniqueness as a person.

If death is the enemy and God's response to it is resurrection,
that means we need not glorify death or affirm the elements in
contemporary funeral practice that can best be described as
corpse-worship. If we really believe in resurrection, then we
can dispose of the dead body in the quickest and simplest fashion and put the emphasis on our good hope.

If Archie had been committed to this belief he could not have
been trapped by Whitehead, who gives him a psychological
arm-twist.

Whitehead. Funerals ain't for the dead, Arch, they're for the living.
Maybe you don't like Oscar but he don't matter now. What
matters now is your neighbors—your friends. Your relatives. The
Man Upstairs. *That* matters. The thing is, Arch, when you walk
away from that cemetery after a Whitehead funeral, you're
gonna hold your head up high.

Arch is bending, but before giving in to the pressure, in one
last desperate attempt he pulls Whitehead aside and asks if he
doesn't have some kind of a special deal like a "used casket or
an old floor model, demonstrator, fleet job—things with nicks,
scratches and tears—whatever."

Whitehead says No and continues to twist. Archie gives in and
pays $975 for a funeral for Cousin Oscar, when all he and Edith
have been able to save over the years is $941.81.

It is sad, but Archie is the victim of his own ignorance and has
been sucked into glorification of death. Now he is the poorer
but perhaps none the wiser, for he knows no alternative to

"Ain't you got any used caskets, old floor models, demonstrators, something cheaper?"

Whitehead's way. That is why I want to share the following with him: the instructions I have set down in the event of my demise. Another person might put them somewhat differently, but the possibility is open to us all.

To My Family

The first person I want you to contact after my death is your pastor. He is equipped to deal with all the problems and needs that will arise in the ensuing hours and days.

One such problem will have to do with what to do with my body. It is my desire that it be used for medical research, and/or, if possible, parts of it used as transplants so that others may live, or see, or function better. It is exciting to me to think my fellow man might be served even in my death.

If this should not be possible I would like my body to be cremated. If the thought of burning bothers you, I want to remind you that you should not think of that body as me. I will have gone on to receive a resurrection body. I consider cremation practical in the light of the fact that in the future there is going to be less and less space for burial. Cremation is also economical, and I have a concern that my dying cause my family as little financial hardship as possible.

Whatever the case, I want my body to be disposed of immediately so it will not need to be embalmed. Neither do I want any cosmetics, viewing, or expensive casket, all of which seem to me to be a denial of the reality of death and of the promise of the resurrection.

Following the committal of my body by you as a family, I would hope there would be a service of Christian worship at the church. The idea of not having the body present for this service is based on the custom of the early Christian Church. Having the body on hand derives from a late custom requiring its presence so that it can be prayed for. I do not believe prayers for the dead to be necessary.

To have this service in a funeral home would be most inappropriate. I am a Christian, and I want my funeral and its location to be expressive of my faith.

The service itself should be a "witness to the resurrection." The theme should be victory.

9

That Unspeakable
Four-Letter Word

Archie was one of the first to introduce us to the use of damns and hells on television. There is one four-letter word, however, which he is very careful not to say. It is the word *love*. Even Edith can't drag it out of him.

Edith. Archie, do you love me?
Archie. Edith, where in the hell are you getting these questions from?''
Edith. *Fiddler on the Roof.* She asks him **(Singing)** ''Do you love me?'' I heard it before on the radio. And the man in the song, he couldn't answer her directly either.
Archie. Well, I ain't no Fiddler on the Roof! I answer that question every day—by the fact that I live with you and take care of you. I go to work and come home, go to work, and come home. . . .

It must be said, in fairness to Archie, that he has once or twice told Edith that he loved her. But the circumstances have to be extreme. One time was when Mike, Gloria, and Edith were all out of town for the weekend, and Archie accidentally locked himself in the basement. The whole incident was quite a fearful thing for him; he envisioned himself dying there of hunger and cold (the latter unalleviated by the furnace, which he had come down to try to repair). In feeling around for some escape, he finds a bottle of old Polish vodka. This not only momentarily warms him up but puts him to sleep, and his fears are transformed into dreams. In his dreaming he does die in the basement, but is able to come back and have one last visit with Edith.

Edith. Archie . . .
Archie. Don't say nothin', Edith.
Edith. You mean you want me to stifle?
Archie. No! Just don't say nothing!
Edith. But why did you bring me down here if you didn't want me to talk to you?
Archie. Now, Edith—I don't want you to get upset or nothin' at what I'm gonna tell you. I mean, this ain't somethin' a man usually tells a woman . . . I—I love you, Edith!
Edith. I know that, Archie.
Archie. You mean I didn't have to say it???! Why don't you never tell me nothin', Edith?

At least he brings himself to utter the word, which is more than he does in everyday life. Listen to him in one of his more romantic moments in the normal course of things.

Archie. Did you ever think of taking a shot at me, Edit'?
Edith. No, Archie.

"I never wanted to shoot you neither."

Archie. That's good. And I never wanted to shoot you neither. It's nice when people get along together. Right, Edit'?

Love is *not* just not wanting to take a shot at someone! Archie seems as confused about love as is the rest of our society. This comes partly from the fact that the word has become so generalized that it is almost meaningless. At one time or another we confuse love with (among other things) attraction, pity, patriotism, indulgence, and that warm feeling some people get when joining hands and singing "Dixie" or the "Battle Hymn of the Republic." We can be heard to say, "I love my sweetheart," "I love my mother," "I love hot-fudge sundaes," "I love my dog,"

"I love little babies," "I love my country," and "I love to walk in the rain."

How mysterious all this would be to a man from Mars, who might easily conclude that anyone saying these various things had exactly the same feeling toward his or her sweetheart, mother, hot-fudge sundaes, and the rest.

Christians complicate the matter even more by saying that "God is love" and that we are to "love our neighbor." The problem is further confused by translation, for in the Greek in which the New Testament was originally written there are several words for love. All except one have in common the understanding that the object loved has something in it that calls forth love from the lover. This is also true of the examples above. There is something in or about each of them that makes you love them. So the love of which we speak is motivated by the object.

It is a "reasonable" love in the sense that the object rouses the lover, enabling him to say, "I love this object *because* it has blue eyes, treats me nicely, tastes good," or whatever. Less specifically we can say, "I love the object because it does something for *me.*" Earthly love is on the whole self-centered, and it is for this reason that charitable organizations have to spend thousands to motivate people to be charitable. This is the aspect that causes Archie's preacher, with dollar signs in his eyes, to quote St. Paul rather one-sidedly: "God loves a cheerful giver"—as if God didn't love grumpy givers or those who do not give at all.

The problem is caused by the self-centeredness of earthly love and our need to find a sufficient motivation in the object. This kind of love has no room for the unlovely; it has no answer for the person who has nothing in or about him or her to arouse love in others. There are many such in our society: the grubby, the dirty, the obnoxious, the hateful, the unattractive. They call for a special kind of love with which we are little familiar. Their only hope is a love that can happen without their furnishing the motivation, or anything about them. This kind of love, for which the Greeks have a word, is something the Bible speaks of and Jesus demonstrated. This *agape* is completely different from love as we ordinarily know it. Let's call it "spiritual love" and compare it to the earthly forms we know.

Earthly love is attracted by the object, while spiritual love has a different source. The former is reasonable, the latter unreasonable and therefore unbelievable. Earthly love says, "I love you because . . ." and gives a reason; spiritual love says "I love you anyway," even when there are reasons for not loving. The one draws into itself and takes, while the other reaches out and gives. Earthly love knows there is a cost to love but expects a certain return, while spiritual love pays the supreme cost, not counting the benefits.

Though many have tried, agape, like God, cannot really be put into words and therefore has to be demonstrated. In Jesus, God was demonstrating his kind of love. Christ came and made friends with outcasts, the unlovables of his day, by giving himself completely. The cross on which he died has become the symbol of agape, so that when we look at that broken, bleeding, thorn-crowned body we remember that God loves like that.

Such love has inspired others who are called Christians to love in the same way. The Bible says the identifying trait of a Christian is love.

This has not, however, been the experience of many non-Christians. Madelyn Murray O'Hare, the renowned atheist, says she has never met a Christian who did not hate her. Coming back to "All in the Family," it would probably be pretty hard to convince Mike that you can recognize Christians by their love, considering the things he has heard one particular person say who calls himself a Christian.

Archie criticizes Mike's going to school by calling him lazy, "The last time I saw him lift a hand around here was to test his deodorant."

He criticizes his nationality, "All her life, the girl waits for 'Mr. Right' and now settles for 'Mr. Wrongski!' "

He criticizes his intelligence with one constantly used word: "Meathead."

Not much love there. It might seem more reasonable to Mike to say you can tell a Christian by his hates.

Others would say you can tell Christians by their fighting, their divisions, their dullness; by their black socks and big Bibles. Yet there have been enough exceptions to give us hope that the day may come when Christians will again be known by their love as they were in the early church.

That will happen when we recognize that God loves us, not because we are lovely or deserving, but because he is love. When we receive him we receive love—the kind I have been trying to describe in these paragraphs.

The Apostle Paul does a better job of describing it in the thirteenth chapter of a letter he wrote to some Christians in the city of Corinth, who were more interested in self-agrandizement than in caring for others. His description is a mini-essay in three parts.

The Value of Love

If I speak in the tongues of men and angels, but have not love, I am a noisy gong or a clanging cymbal.

"Love is not arrogant or rude."

And if I have prophetic powers, and understand all mysteries and all knowledge, and if I have all faith, so as to remove mountains, but have not love, I am nothing.

The speaking in tongues, prophetic powers, mountain-moving faith, etc., were all part of a game the Christians of Corinth were playing, called "spiritual one-upmanship." Paul checkmates the game by saying, "If you don't have love, don't waste your time."

The game did not die with the Corinthians. Many of us still try to score with different forms of religious ostentation and personal pretensions. Look at Archie's claim to Mike the night Archie decided they were going to say grace before dinner.

Archie. We gotta thank God for this food which comes from God.
Mike. How about askin' him to lower his prices.

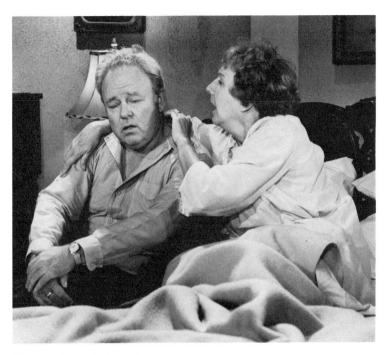

"Love endures all things."

Archie. Stop that there blasphemy! This here is a Christian God-fearin' home, and when you're sittin' at this table, you're gonna be just as afraid of God as the rest of us! Now everybody clam up and bow your heads.

Sounds pretty religious. But it also sounds like a noisy gong and a clanging cymbal because it lacks love.

The Nature of Love

Love is patient and kind; love is not jealous or boastful; it is not arrogant or rude. Love does not insist on its own way; it is not irritable or resentful; it does not rejoice at wrong, but rejoices in the right. Love bears all things, believes all things, hopes all things, endures all things.

Words like "patient," "kind," "not arrogant or rude" judge the Archie in all of us. But the amazing thing about these words is that they describe Edith. She is all of them, and that's why she is so lovable.

Love's Endurance

Love never ends; as for prophecies, they will pass away; as for tongues, they will cease; as for knowledge, it will pass away. . . . So faith, hope, love abide, these three; but the greatest of these is love. Make love your aim.

You see, Archie, love is more than not wanting to take a shot at someone.

A lot more.

10

Archie and the Church

Archie wasn't as happy about youth winning the right to vote as other members of the household. His response was a sarcastic. "Whoopee! Youth is voting! 'And a little child shall lead them.' Whoever said that didn't know nothing."

Not realizing it was the prophet Isaiah who said that, or how explicitly Jesus himself made our entering the kingdom of God dependent on our receiving it "like a child," Archie gives us a clue to his background knowledge of the Christian faith, which seems directly proportionate to his church attendance. He has what Bishop Pike called a "sprinkling relationship" to the church, referring to those whose only contact with it is when they are sprinkled with water at baptism, sprinkled with rice at marriage, and sprinkled with earth at death. Archie may attend a Mothers' Day or Easter service now and then, but he is really not too excited about church or his pastor Rev. Fletcher, whom he calls "Bleedin' Heart Felcher."

I think if you were to ask Archie he would tell you he doesn't need the Church, and he may have good reason for saying so.

Especially if "Felcher" is as bad a preacher as he makes out. On one of his rare visits he finds he can't stomach Fletcher's sermon and leaves in the middle of it.

Archie. That was socialist propaganda, pure and simple. And don't look at me like that. And I'm not sittin' still for no preacher blamin' me for all this here breakdown in law and order. The cause of it is all those sob sisters like the Reverend Felcher . . . half a sermon was plenty. He said all he was gonna say.

Archie may have some legitimate complaints. There is nothing worse than a long-winded preacher who keeps on going after he has said all he has to say. Nor can I defend one who gets his kicks from verbally beating up on people week after week because of their lack of social concern. Such haranguing may come out of deep compassion for the underdog, but it accomplishes little besides alienating and polarizing people's feeling. They don't enjoy being told what is wrong with them. Yet there are ways of helping them to recognize the problems of our society, the degree to which they are a part of the problem, and how they can become a part of the answer. That is the function and responsibility of the effective clergyman.

You also have to be a little suspect of Fletcher's church when you observe Edith's church activities. She is the kind of human who will respond to the biggest challenge the Church has to offer. Yet her "major activity" in it is serving tea to the ladies at church socials.

Archie says he doesn't need the Church. And if it is no more than long-winded sermons, verbal punishment, and holy tea parties you have to agree with him. But if the church was just the way Archie wanted it, what would it be like?

Let's suppose that Archie has become a major influence in the church, and under his leadership changes have come about. Let's make a Sunday morning visit. They still have worship at eleven o'clock on Sunday morning (only), which may be the most inconvenient time of the week but does give everyone a chance to milk their cows and do other farm chores, the reason such a time was chosen in the first place. As we meet other folks arriving, we note that they all look as if they were in uniform, the ladies in "proper clothes" and the men in white shirts and dark ties. They all seem to agree with Archie's dictum: "I don't want to face my Lord without a white shirt and tie." Don't doubt Archie's sincerity here; he is so committed to the concept that he has had to miss church some Sundays because he didn't have a clean white shirt.

Going into the church, we are surprised to see that the pews have been replaced by rocking chairs, and everybody rocks together as they sing what Archie calls the *old* hymns—which he has never noticed were written in the early part of this century, long after most of the others in the hymnbook.

No one seems to pay much attention to the words, which speak of "Ebenezer," "soldiers," "bloody fountains," and "Mount Pisgah's lofty heights." You have the feeling you had better not ask any questions about them for fear of the embarrassing silence that would follow.

Remembering that during Rev. Fletcher's day they used guitars in worship, I ask the person next to me what happened to them, to which she replies: "Thanks to the leadership of Mr. Bunker we got rid of those terribly modern instruments" (such as David played in the Old Testament) "and now we just have the traditional organ" (which David never heard of, since it was invented after his time and not used by the Church until the fifth century).

After the singing they receive the offering by asking everyone to insert their credit cards into the mechanism attached to the back of the rocker in front of them.

Next there is a flag salute, led by Archie, which causes me to bother my neighbor again: "But isn't the church universal?" Her answer is terse, "Yes, and so is America." The sermon that follows is short. A couple of pithy sayings and a poem by Edgar Guest. Then they sing their favorite closing hymn.

> We'll build a sweet little nest
> Somewhere in the West,
> And let the rest of the world go by.

Archie would probably prefer to say "And let the rest of the world go to hell," but might not quite dare. There are some elements of irony here. For if indeed the Church should ever really become a sweet little nest for rocking-chair Christians, then the world will literally go to hell.

Jesus died for the world, and God's people must live for it and its redemption.

It may be that both Fletcher and Bunker have become victims of what psychologist Hobert Mower calls the Church's "institutional detour." The Church (here I am not speaking of a building but of people sharing life together in relationship with each other and with God) was established to carry out the mission of Christ and to fill some basic needs of people. When those needs are not met by the Church, we attempt to fulfill them in other ways and places, which usually turn out to be pretty poor substitutes.

One of man's basic needs is for fellowship. We were not made to be alone. We need people to whom we can relate, with whom we have some sense of community, and on whom we can depend for acceptance and support. The New Testament Church was made up of such people. Archie has not found them in his local church and has had to look elsewhere, which explains why he missed dinner one night. Edith lets us know how significant this is when she says, "It must really be something. The only other time Archie ever missed dinner was once when he slept through it."

What could have been so important as to make Archie miss dinner and arrive home late *singing?* Even Edith is mystified.

Edith. Archie! Are you all right?

Archie. That's why I'm singing! I'm all right! I'm terrific. The greatest thing in my life happened today.

Edith. That's wonderful! What is it?

Archie. It's sensational! Are you ready?

Edith. I can hardly wait.

Archie. Hank Phillips is dead.

Edith. Oh my.

Mike. A man dies and you're happy.

Archie. Wait a minute, will ya. I ain't happy 'cause he died. I'm happy 'cause he can't bowl no more. You see, I've been waiting six years to get on this team and now there's an opening. . . . I'm trying for the greatest bowling team in the league—the Cannonballers.

As he continues to talk we discover that the Cannonballers are a religion for Archie. When Moose comes by to take him to meet the team he asks:

Moose. Well, Arch, are you all set for tonight?

Archie. "Am I all set? I got my ball all polished, new laces for my shoes . . . I tell you Moose, you got no idea how much this means

"The Cannonballers is only the best team in the league."

to me. Not only bowling with you guys but I'm looking forward
to those monthly smokers I been hearing about.

Moose. Arch, the monthly smokers—that's a Cannonballer secret.
Who told you about that, Arch?

Archie. Hank Phillips.

Moose. Oh. He coulda been kicked out for that. Lucky for him he's
dead.

Secrets have long been a part of many religions. Moreover,
Archie gets ready for bowling as he gets ready for church, and
he admits it is the fellowship and acceptance that is significant
to him. Later he describes what it was like that night.

Archie. I'm so nervous I'm sweatin' bullets and just as I'm about to
bowl, Moose comes over and he does the nicest thing in the
world. He puts his arm around me and says, "Easy, Arch. Don't
get your bowels in an uproar." Well, a thing like that gives a guy
courage.

Another ingredient of true religion, supportive encouragement.

We need identity, and any good religion provides it, as the
Cannonballers attempt to do with bowling shirts. We saw Archie's ecstasies back on p. 36: ". . . the bowling shirts them
Cannonballers got. All yellow silk, with bright red piping. . . .
on the back . . . a picture of a cannon firing a bowling ball.
. . . Beautiful. When you got something like that on your back
. . . you know you're somebody."

Identity!

The Cannonballers' religion even has a heaven.

Archie. Did I tell you about the big annual banquet the Cannonballers throw? . . . They rent out the American Legion Hall in
Mineola, which is beautiful. And then they come and pick you
up here right in front of the house on a big chartered bus . . .
takes you out there first class all the way. They put a case of beer
on the bus, and to work up a thirst they pass out them big Jewish
pretzels. And if that ain't enough, when you get to the hall, wow
—they've got a big fancy spread for us. All the cold cuts and
salad you can shove into yourselves. And then after that feast I
step up and get my trophy.

Heaven is that big annual Cannonballers' banquet in the sky.

That's a lot to get from a bowling team—secrets, fellowship,
acceptance, supportive encouragement, identity, and heaven—
though all are poor models of the real thing.

The secrets are nothing when compared to the secrets or
mysteries of God revealed in Jesus Christ. The fellowship is
surface and exclusive as opposed to that depth-sharing life for
all men found in the New Testament Church. The acceptance
is predicated on how well you bowl and probably your attitudes
toward various things, as opposed to the "whosoever will" invitation of Jesus. Supportive encouragement may be present on
bowling night, but next morning Moose will be another of Archie's competitors on the job. Jesus promises, "Lo, I am with you
always."

The Cannonballers' identity is shed as easily as taking off a
bowling shirt. Our identity is described in Scripture as the eternal one of being "God's own people."

Heaven annually? The Bible promises that we can begin life
that is eternal in both quality and quantity, right now.

It is sad if the Cannonballers are the best Archie's world has

"Archie and his priest."

to offer, and the really pathetic moment comes when he hears that he didn't make the team after all. What does Archie do? He "goes to church" at Kelsey's Tavern. He partakes of his sacraments, beer instead of wine, pretzels for bread, and pours out his heart to Kelsey, the priest. Kelsey listens to him, understands him, and encourages him before sending him out into the world alone so that he can lock up.

The expression on Archie's face as he leaves the tavern and moves into the darkness speaks from the depths of his soul. It says, "If only I could find a church that had the camaraderie of a bowling team and the sympathy of a tavern."

11

Archie and the Bible

Archie belongs to that large segment of people who will fight to the death for the Bible but seldom if ever read it. Though most of its pages are for him unknown territory, he is not reticent when it comes to interpreting the Bible to others or using it as a weapon to put down anyone who disagrees with him. One feels that he will seldom reach for a Bible to illustrate his views unless he is going to be reading from Genesis, which, being the first book, is easy to find.

He decides to give Mike and Gloria a science lesson from Scripture.

Archie. "And the rib which the Lord God had taken from man made he a woman and brought her unto the man. And Adam said this is now bone of my bones and flesh of my flesh: she shall be called woman because she was taken out of man." There it is in black and white! So we *didn't* crawl out from under the rocks and we *didn't* have tails, and we wasn't a bunch of monkeys neither, you atheistic pinko meathead you.

"We *didn't* crawl out from under the rocks and we *didn't* have tails."

Mike. Archie, that was written in the dark ages. The whole idea of taking a rib out of Adam and making a woman—it's Mandrake the Magician time.

Archie. Edith! Did you hear what I heard? This meathead's comparing God with Mandrake the Magician. Can you believe it?

Edith. No, God is much better known.

Archie. Listen, I give up on you two! Maybe you come from monkeys and baboons, but I was made by God in his own image.

Mike. You mean God looks like *you?*

Archie. I didn't mean there was an exact resemblance, I mean he made us perfect like himself, that's what I mean.

Mike. Perfect?

Archie. Yes, perfect . . . No, I don't mean perfect that way . . . I
mean . . . I got faults, I'm not saying I ain't. None of us is perfect.
What I mean is—he made us with—well—four fingers and one
thumb on each hand. He even thought of that, two hands.
Because he knew one hand wasn't going to be good enough.
And he put them at the end of your arms where they'd be most
handy . . .

Edith. That's why they're called hands, I suppose.

Thus the interpretation of the biblical story of the creation of
man according to Archie Bunker. He asks no questions about
the kind of material he is dealing with, nor does he consider that
truth may be found in other places. He has never really studied
the Bible, yet speaks as an authority.

The above is about the only reference I happen to have heard
Archie make to the Bible except the time he was defending
miracles to Mike:

Mike. There is no such thing as miracles.

Archie. Not to you, but to decent people who read the Bible there's
a lot of miracles . . . What about Noah and the whale? And look
at Samson who took a jawbone of a little ass and slew the whole
army of the Philippines.

If I were to meet Archie at a cocktail party, I am sure he
would fall into the pattern of the many others who, on discovering I am a clergyman, feel constrained to say something religious—if possible, something that will show their high degree
of familiarity with the Bible. They are usually nonchalant. Helping themselves to an extra *hors d'oeuvre*, they will turn to me,
"Like the Bible says, 'God helps those who help themselves.'

"God is much better known than Mandrake the Magician."

Right, Reverend?" I don't know who said that, but it wasn't the Bible. Nor do I know how to respond to the question, so I usually just smile.

If there is a crowd around, and the person has no guilt over the *hors d'oeuvres*, he tries a little theological one-upmanship on me, softened with a bit of humor of course, and asks so all may hear, "Reverend, I bet you don't know where in the Bible it says a man can have sixteen wives."

He is right, I don't, and so I ask him where.

"Four better, four worse, four richer, and four poorer."

Again the least embarrassing thing I can think of doing is to grin politely, for that is not in the Bible either. I take it he has heard it at somebody's wedding ceremony.

This is about as deep as biblical discussions get for the average person. There are those, however, who are much more serious about the Bible yet greatly misuse it. There is the legend of the man out in wild bush country who, believing it to be good alike for soul and body, ate two pages daily with seemingly no side effects until he was poisoned by the ink from the colored pictures.

The Gideons, committed to the distribution of Bibles, tell us that among convicts who do not read it there are still some who find its thin pages useful for rolling cigarettes.

Other folk are just plain awed by Scripture, like the man who took time to count the words in the King James version. He found 773,693. For an encore he counted the letters—3,539,489.

Archie's Bible was presented to him by the government during World War II. It was one of 11,000,000 bought and given away by the Army to help build the morale of the troops. No one knows how many of them were read, or how many were to their owners nothing more than a spiritual rabbit's foot.

Like many of us, Archie would be hard put to it to say what the Bible really is. The possible answers, gleaned from observing people's attitudes, are endless: a science book, a spiritual good-luck piece, a "paper Pope," a paperweight, a book of magic, an attractive ornament, a "lovely book," a divine Ouiji board, the Word of God, the Holy Book, and so on. Yet some sort of true answer to the question is important to insure proper use of the Bible—just as important—to make sure that we don't misuse it. For me the most meaningful answers are those given by three great theologians: Martin Luther, Søren Kierkegaard and Emil Brunner.

"The Manger of Christ" is Martin Luther's description of this ancient Book, or library of books. A manger contains straw, which may be the words of men; but this Manger also contains Christ, who is the true word of God. It is quite worth our while to dig through the straw of cultural hang-ups and old superstitions to discover the Living Word, Jesus Christ.

"God's Love Letter" is Kierkegaard's definition. This means that the Bible is personal and relational. A love letter is never an end; it is a means by which two beings communicate, share, and get to know each other more deeply. A love letter in some miraculous way expresses what can never really be put into words—the love of one person for another. So it is with God's Love Letter. In it we discover, in penetrating and poignant ways, the Good News that we are loved by God.

"His Master's Voice" is Emil Brunner's answer to the question, taking us back to the old ad of a dog listening, fascinated, to the sound of a Victrola. If you have heard an old phonograph you know that you hear more than a voice: scratches, static, and cracks are also amplified. But these are not what has the dog's attention. It is his master's voice. So it is with the Bible. Many people have read Scripture off and on for years, sidetracked and bothered by the scratches and static, yet there are those who one day hear something more—the Master's voice—and their lives are changed as for them the Bible becomes the Word of God.

In a day when public cautions are printed on everything from cigarettes to aspirin, I should like to follow suit by putting one on the cover of the Bible. It would read:

WARNING

The intent of this book is always to point beyond itself to the God who loves you. Do not allow it to become an end in itself. That would be idolatry.

Rather, read the Bible looking for Christ, feeling for love, and listening for God.

12

The Ten Commandments

"My religion is simple," says Archie. "The Ten Commandments, that's my religion. I call 'em the 'Big Ten' and I keep 'em too."

Nothing wrong with this as a standard, but when people tell me that they live by the Ten Commandments I always want to ask how they are doing on the first one. Remember? "Thou shalt have no other gods before me."

A god is whatever comes first in our lives, whatever takes that number one position which rightfully belongs to God the Heavenly Father. Most of us put ourselves in that first place, but self is not the only candidate. Just about any thing or idea that ever existed has been somebody's god, be it an idol carved out of a stick of wood or a granite cathedral which, by its very art, steals the devotion that rightfully belongs to the God for whose worship it was raised.

Among the idols of Archie Bunker is one that stands high above the rest: the god of nationalism. When you hear Archie speak of "God and country" you wonder if he knows the difference. If he does, it still seems that he considers them equal. This close relationship of the two in his mind comes out in a conversation with Mike.

Archie. It ain't a question of sides. God is always on the side of right.

Mike. And we are always right?

Archie. Well, of course we are! You don't expect them Godless Gooks to be right, do you?

Mike. How can those Gooks be Godless, Archie, when God created them?

Archie. God didn't create them, smart guy! It was the devil that created them.

Not only do his country and God seem to have a unique relationship, but Archie claims for the nation the attributes of God by asserting that it, too, is always right.

This may be the worst thing about his idolatrous form of nationalism: placing the nation on a par with God by claiming it to be perfect. Such smugness is the very thing that leads to the destruction of nations, as we see in the biblical story of the Tower of Babel in Genesis 11. Here man tries to build, through his own skills, a tower "with its top in the heavens" as a symbol of his pride. But God, we are told, came down to see it, and from that time forth human language was confused and the people, who had been a single people, scattered. The very object that might have been an expression of unity became the vehicle of disorder and separation.

Up to this point in Genesis the Bible has spoken to individual men and women. Here in the story of the Tower of Babel collective humanity is addressed for the first time, and warning is given to all groups or nations that their existence is depen-

"Of course, God is on our side."

dent upon God. They must never see themselves as the final answer, nor demand from humanity the allegiance that belongs to God.

Archie says it truly in the flag salute, "One nation *under*

God," but he doesn't mean it. He continually puts his country on a level with God, which prevents him from recognizing any need for change, improvement, or renewal. Worse still, his basic premise forces him to defend some pretty indefensible things.

Mike. What do you mean—America: Love it or leave it?

Archie. That's right, it's a free country, so amscray.

Mike. But what would our leaving solve? With or without protesters we'd still have the same problems.

Archie. What problems?

Mike. The war. The race problem. The economic problem. The pollution problem.

Archie. Well, if you're gonna nitpick.

Anything we put above criticism is our idol. Archie not only worships his country, but America has become a religion to him, a religion without ideas or ideals. It is made up of elements which in a weird sort of way unite his nationalism with another god called materialism. He speaks of this Siamese-twin deity in what might be called his creedal statement:

Archie. There's three great things that happens to a man in his lifetime. Buying a house . . . a car . . . and a new color TV. That's what America is all about.

We discover on one occasion that Archie's materialistic dreams go further. The possibility arises that he may be able to sell their house to a "blockbuster" for $35,000. If he can complete the deal he will then move to his paradise, El Monte, California, and live on sunshine and orange juice. Further observation shows us that Archie's two-headed god of nationalism and materialism also includes his Queens home (to which he escapes every night), his chair (in which he sits, in front of his color TV, to enjoy those mini-worship services called commercials), the baseball bat in his bedroom for household security, an ultimate trip to Disneyland, and of course his hero and high priest, John Wayne.

Nearly three thousand years ago David the psalmist expressed his faith in God in flowing words still tenderly, hauntingly familiar to a large fraction of the world.

> The Lord is my shepherd, I shall not want; he makes me lie
>   down in green pastures.
> He leads me beside still waters; he restores my soul.
> He leads me in paths of righteousness for his name's sake.
> Even though I walk through the valley of the shadow of
>   death, I fear no evil; for thou art with me; thy rod and thy
>   staff, they comfort me.
> Thou preparest a table before me in the presence of mine
>   enemies; thou anointest my head with oil, my cup overflows.
> Surely goodness and mercy shall follow me all the days of my
>   life; and I shall dwell in the house of the Lord for
> ever.(Psalm 23 RSV)

Archie would not be able honestly to quote the above without some paraphrasing in the interest of his own personal religion. One might guess something along these lines:

> Uncle Sam is my shepherd, I shall not want; he makes me sit
>   down in my big easy chair.
> He leads me in front of the color TV; why worry about my soul?
> He leads me in the paths of the supermarket for my own sake.
> Yea, though I walk through the minefields of the Queens

subways, I will fear no evil; for John Wayne is with me;
my baseball bat and his gun comfort me.

Thou preparest a place for me far from the presence of
mine enemies, in El Monte, California; thou anointest
my head with sunshine; my orange juice runneth over.

Surely money and gadgets shall follow me all the days of
my life, and I will dwell in or near Disneyland forever.

The Ten Commandments are a great standard, but when we take them seriously they turn around and judge us, as Archie is judged by the first one. But he does not stand alone. Idolatry is rampant and false gods abound in our world. Take your choice: self, money, pleasure, sex, romance, amusement, sports, education, power, comfort, and so forth. None is bad in itself; all are bad when they usurp the central place of God. Take your pick, choose your god, bet your bottom dollar on it. But be warned! These gods cannot give you the life and freedom for which we all hunger. There is only one who can give these: God our Creator. He gives us freedom and life, and then, to preserve and protect them, he gives the Ten Commandments.

13

One Down, Nine To Go

It was just like one of those long interview-dialogues you read in so many magazines these days. Except this one was between Archie Bunker and Spencer Marsh. I'm glad we recorded it,* and I am happy to share it with you. I found Archie to be both sincere and at times tender almost to the point of timidity, though I was a little disappointed that we never got much beyond the surface. Each time I felt we were getting to the meat of something, Archie would move us on to the next commandment.

Archie. Geez, ya sure made a big deal outa it when I said my religion was the Ten Commandments. You jumped on me with that first commandment like I was some kinda Commie pinko or somethin'.

S. M. I'm sorry if I came down too hard. I've had some pet idols of

*With Archie's permission, on a recorder in full view—I have no "bugged" Bibles or the like.

my own that keep trying to sneak back into my life, and the only way I can keep them out is by taking the first commandment seriously.

Archie. I understand that, but I don't understand what you meant when you said, "The Ten Commandments pertect and perserve freedom and life." Don't misunderstand me. I'm not a freedom nut. I think we got too much freedom already. But how do laws or commandments pertect freedom?

S. M. Let me put it this way. I live near some high cliffs bordering the ocean. At the top there is a beautiful park. Sounds like a crazy place for a park—who would want to run and play in a park on the edge of a cliff—who would dare? Well, the answer to that is, just about everybody. Because there's a big fence at the edge, so we're perfectly safe running around and playing in the park. It's true, there are a few places we'd like to break through now and then, but this fence not only keeps us from danger but gives us real freedom inside the grounds. God's laws are the same. They both hold us back and leave us free. I believe keeping them insures our freedom, and breaking them destroys it. Do you see what I mean?

Archie. Yeah, I think so. Like, the fences help to keep out the devil. The other thing is—you oughta know even tho' I didn't rate too well on that first one, I don't do so bad on the rest.

S. M. Shall we talk about those?

Archie. Yeah, go ahead.

S. M. How about the next one?

Archie. Well, how about it?

S. M. "You shall not make any graven image."

Archie. That's for those jungle people and the Catholics, right?

S. M. I'm not so sure. Maybe we'd better talk about what these commandments mean for me and you. Like I think this commandment is the reverse side of the first, which says we shouldn't raise things up to the level of God. I think it warns us about bringing God down to the level of things. I suppose that's the reason I'm a little bothered when I hear you and other people call him "the Man Upstairs." That shrinks him to our level. He's much more than a man.

Archie. I think I see what ya mean, but I don't know for sure if I mean what you think I mean. Anyway, is the next one about the Lord thy God's name in vain?

S. M. Yes.

Archie. I'm guilty. But if you worked with the clowns I work with and had a meathead for a son-in-law you'd be guilty, too. Besides, I bet you slip now and then. How 'bout it, preacher?

S. M. I try not to use God's name as profanity, but I'm more concerned, to tell the truth, about taking his name "in vain" when I use it too easily. I think one way of stating this commandment would be to say, "When you use God's name, use it seriously." As a preacher I sometimes find myself mentioning God in a ritualistic way that's almost meaningless. I believe it's wrong to use his name and not be in earnest. It's a potential sin of us all, but especially preachers and politicians.

Archie. Right, so be sure you watch it. *(He chuckles)* What's the next one?

S. M. "Remember the Sabbath and keep it holy."

Archie. That one's outdated except for Jews. Right?

S. M. Well, let's say, half right. The early Christians changed the day of worship from the Sabbath or Saturday (beginning Friday night) to the Lord's Day, Sunday, so they could celebrate Easter or the Resurrection every week. I think they still kept the spirit of this commandment since it still has the rhythm of one out of seven.

We all need such a rhythm of work and rest.

Archie. Are you one of these guys who think we shouldn't do anything on Sundays but go to church?

S. M. No, I think we can keep the rhythm a lot of ways, and Sunday is a great day for rest and for play, especially when we see play as a celebration of the life God has given us. But at the same time, I have to say that regular worship can be a profound, uplifting, and life-giving experience.

Archie. But it gets to be such a big deal with the time it takes for dressin' up and then dressin' down again.

S. M. You're right. But who says you have to dress up? Maybe we should rethink that idea.

Archie. I'd rather not go to church at all if I can't go dressed up.

S. M. Haven't you ever heard that it is what is on the inside of us that God is concerned about?

Archie. Yeah, but how d'ya know he's ever goin' to look inside if he don't like the outside?

S. M. Come on, Archie!

Archie. Well . . . it's a thought. What's the next one?

S. M. Well, we've looked at the first four, which deal with our relation to God. The other six deal with our relation to our fellow man. The fifth concerns itself with preserving the family: "Honor your Father and Mother."

Archie. Now that's one worth repeating. All you hear about today is the rights of kids. Us parents has got some rights too.

S. M. I agree, Archie. I have a real desire that my children honor me, but at the same time I want to remember two things. To be an honorable parent, and not to forget all the aged parents of our nation, many of whom are living in pretty dishonorable conditions.

Archie. Yeah, yeah. What's next?

S. M. What's the hurry? Don't you want to talk about what I just said?

Archie. No, 'cause I know where you're tryin' to lead me and we got enough welfare already. What's next?

S. M. "Thou shalt not kill."

Archie. I never killed anybody.

S. M. I haven't either, at least not directly.

Archie. Whaddya mean, "not directly"?

S. M. I think you've heard before that some of us feel when our tax dollars pay for bombs to kill, that somehow makes us part of the killing. And there are other ways to kill. We kill each other on our highways, and we kill ourselves with excess eating, over- work, booze, tobacco, and drugs. I don't know, Archie—I don't think we've taken this commandment very seriously.

Archie. Maybe not. When we goin' to talk about that adultery one?

S. M. That's next. "Thou shalt not commit adultery."

Archie. I tried to explain that one to Edit'. I told her, "You gotta take into account men's hormones." I told her I couldn't get into it too deep. It's too male, see, and it's too rough. But when his hormones is acting up, I wouldn't trust any man as far as I can throw him. You know what she said? "But then that would include you, Archie." I told her, "Not necessarily. Because I don't let my hormones act up." I believe that commandment.

S. M. I do too. It's a beautiful commandment because it assures the privacy and sacredness of intimacy in marriage. There may be no more beautiful words for a man or a woman to hear than the words, "I love only you."

Archie. You know, I think I understand what you were saying about fences—I kept this commandment but I don't feel fenced in. I'm havin' an experience some guys have fenced theirselves out of. With Edit' it's Archie only and with me it's Edit' only.

"With me, it is Edit' only."

S. M. You've got it, Archie, don't lose it. The next one is "Thou shalt not steal."

Archie. I bet that's the most broken one of all.

S. M. How do you mean?

Archie. I mean all these burglaries and holdups and stuff.

S. M. They are terrible, Archie, but you know they say much more money is stolen from banks by the "respectable employees" than by holdup men you can see. And there are so many ways of stealing, like cheating on your income tax, padding your expense account, reporting as lost the tools you have taken home, withholding a fair wage, or not doing the amount and quality of work that's paid for. I think you're right, Archie, this may be the one we break most—except for the next one: "You shall not bear false witness."

Archie. Does that mean lyin'?

S. M. Yes.

Archie. But little white lies is OK.

S. M. I don't know if a lie can be little when you consider the ability lies have to multiply themselves and the way they all fit together in a growing cancer of untruth that seems to be spreading across our society. Have you ever thought what it would be like to live in a world where nobody can believe anybody? It's eerie, and I'm afraid we're headed that way unless some of us will commit ourselves to the truth at all times, in all places.

Archie. I don't know. I don't think people need to know everything.

S. M. I don't either, but I don't think that's the same as giving false information. I affirm the right to privacy, but I don't think lying is the way to protect it. I also want to say that the happiest, healthiest people I know are the open, honest ones.

Archie. You mean, like Edit'?

S. M. Yes, like Edith.

Archie. Is that all the commandments?

S. M. No, one more: "Thou shalt not covet."

Archie. What's "covet"?

S. M. That's hard to answer. You could call it desire out of control, or the evil desire to have what is not ours, or just plain greed. It's a summary of all the other commandments, since they are usually by-products of covetousness. This is the sin that is fed by Madison Avenue and slowly shrivels our souls.

Archie. OK, Preacher, you made your point. So I don't keep all the commandments, exactly. But who does?

That's just the point, Archie, nobody does. The Ten Commandments give us a great standard but also judge us. They are the fences that protect us from the abyss beyond the cliff. But there is something in us that makes us want to jump fences. Once we go over the fence and are roaming around the crumbling edges of the cliffs, we're headed for destruction, our only hope being the miracle of a Savior swooping down and catching us before we hit bottom. That's exactly what God has done for us in Jesus Christ. We call it Good News, the good news that first came from an angel who said, "For unto *you* is born this day . . . a Savior, who is Christ the Lord."

14

Religiosity

Every time Archie has a "scrape with God" he becomes more religious. This we saw when a ton crate of machine parts fell off the crane at work and missed him by inches. Though Mike raised the possibility that God may have been trying to hit Archie and missed, Archie was convinced it was God's doing that he escaped. The crate fell close enough to scare a little religion into him, which he seems to think is not only a panacea for himself but for the whole world.

Archie. I tell you my heart goes out to a lot of guys I know. They spend all their lives belonging to one of them anything-goes religions. They raise their kids in it, they give money to it, they run dances for it . . . only to get up there someday and find out they was foolin' around with the wrong one all the time! It's sad, you know that?

I have to say that being "religious," no matter what the form of it, is not going to solve man's predicament. Neither do I believe it is God's intention that we be religious, if this means mainly a commitment to certain creeds, systems, laws, and doctrines. Such religion, while comfortable for many, so often does just the opposite of what God wants to have happen in our lives. Pursuing this for a moment:

God intends us to be free, but religion frequently binds us.

God intends us to be humble, but religion often creates a kind of smugness in those who are its closest adherents.

God intends us to live in unity with our fellow man, but religion too often divides us into camps of orthodox, heretic, and infidel.

God intends us to love and be of service to our fellow man, but religion can get us so involved with its own "holy" and ecclesiastical games that no time is left for the real thing.

These sentences are the words of a struggler who, having felt the weight and squeeze of religion, has had to see it as *not* the answer. But I am by no means the first to make that discovery. The Old Testament prophet Amos was so convinced of the inadequacies of "religion" that he moves in on it like a mighty bulldozer, speaking for God in one of the boldest strokes against narrowly formal and empty religion to be found anywhere.

> I hate, I despise your feasts,
>   and I take no delight in your solemn assemblies.
> Even though you offer me your burnt offerings . . .
>   I will not accept them,
> And the peace offerings of your fatted beasts
>   I will not look upon.
> Take away from me the noise of your songs;
>   to the melody of your harps I will not listen.
> But let justice roll down like waters,
>   and righteousness like an everflowing stream.

Amos makes clear that God is not interested in religious games. His concern is for justice, or right relationships between men; and righteousness, which means to be right with God. The people did not listen to Amos but continued to play their games unheeding, while justice and righteousness disappeared from among them. In the end, these "religious" people were destroyed.

Jesus illustrates the point even more clearly. His anger was most often triggered by religious people, some of whom he referred to as "whited sepulchres"—bright on the outside but on the inside, dead men's bones.

In the eyes of many Jesus was irreligious, for he readily went against religious ordinances when they seemed to get in the way of urgent need, or were otherwise relatively unimportant. In the end the religious people were among those who killed him. Their nationality is not significant; the fact that they were religious is.

Following Jesus' death and resurrection, his Church was established. Here was a real chance to see how Jesus' form of "unreligion" would work, for the Church was, no more and no less, a group of people who had a deep relationship with one another, centered in their relation to God through Jesus. Some members of the new community, while drawn to the person of Jesus, still could not leave their old observances behind. And like so many of us, they started trying to put their thing onto everyone else.

The story is told in the fifteenth chapter of the Book of Acts. It concerns Paul and Barnabas, excited over the number of Gentiles who were joining the new community. But those who were still unable to get unhooked from their old ideas reacted with disdain. They insisted that Gentiles should not be accepted until they had fulfilled the requirements of the Law; they were trying to turn this beautiful relational community into an organized, formulated religion focused on the Law.

This was the very thing from which Peter had found freedom. With a kind of "don't-send-me-back-to-prison" cry, he pleaded with them not to put on the backs of new members what they themselves had not been able to handle: "the unbearable yoke of religion" (the Scripture actually uses the word *law*, but "religion" is a fair paraphrase). Peter had found something better than formal religion; he had found life, and was not going back to the old yoke. He was drinking deep of the peace, the joy, and the abundant life he had discovered since knowing Jesus—that Jesus who calls us not to "religion" but to relationship.

That is the word we must rediscover and hold onto: *relationship*. Our need and God's plan for our wholeness is right relationships. This is what the new community established by Jesus had—they were people in right relationship with God, self, and others.

As I noted earlier, I have tried the narrowly "religious" route and it almost destroyed me. I found it inhibiting, binding, and debilitating, but when I discovered that God was calling me not to religion but to relationship, and began to live the relational life, I was liberated.

I started living by asking myself just what was my relation to God, self, and others. How did they feel about me, and how did I feel about them?

God. How did God feel about me? Trying to be honest, I had to admit that for most of my life I had somehow felt that God for some reason was provoked at me. If I was smart I would try to stay out of his way. And I felt I was succeeding, except for a few intermittent times of real hardship which I considered to be God's punishment.

Then I ran into a group of Christians who told me that my conclusions were correct: God was mad at me, and he had a right to be. They said if I was really smart I would get Jesus on my side to appease him. So in prayer I asked Jesus to help me, with the hope that he would be adequate protection from the God of wrath. This gave me some sense of security, but not enough to keep me from playing the religious game that I hoped would make God like me. I played it for many years before I came to the realization that the Gospel—the Good News—was not that God is mad at me, yet can be appeased (that would be essentially bad news). The Good News is that God loves me.

It is unbelievable but true. God loves me.

And he doesn't want me to hide from him in fear. Rather, he wants me to allow him to love me.

Self. If I am loved by God, then I must begin to see myself as someone of tremendous value. It enabled me to begin to love myself, whom I must have disliked pretty deeply considering how I treated myself: the kind of stuff I put into my body, the general lack of physical care, with no real attention to my psychological needs, and but worst of all my deliberate spiritual self-hatred. I became part of "Christian" groups who spent their time beating up on themselves in the name of Christian humility. For these people the epitome of commitment was to be able to say, "I am nothing."

My new knowledge delivered me from such foolishness. If God loves me I am not nothing. I am a tremendous someone.

Others. Knowing I was loved by God has freed me to love myself, and now, loving myself, to love others. I saw that Jesus' command that we should love others could not be fulfilled until we love ourselves. His words, "Love your neighbor as yourself" verify this. But once we do that we are really free to love others.

Now it all fit. I could see that I was my most hateful when I loved myself least, and I loved myself least when I felt least loved by God. People from whom I have had hate in life, I discovered, were those who didn't really love themselves, and I was able to help them know their own value by loving them. Then they began to love me and others because their self-centeredness, which produced their hate, was turned into high regard for self that produced love.

You see, Archie, it's not "religion," it's relationship. Have you ever wondered why you dislike so many people? Isn't it because you yourself don't really like Archie? And the reason for that is that you don't understand how much you are loved— God loves you! Edith loves you! And you know something funny? Now that I've come to know you and can see the struggles, hurts, and dreams behind all that noise, gruffness, and bigotry, I have come to love you too.

The photographs on the preceding pages picture the following performers:

Carroll O'Connor	*as*	Archie Bunker
Jean Stapleton		Edith Bunker
Rob Reiner		Michael Stivic
Sally Struthers		Gloria Stivic

Additionally, appearing on:

Page